PRAISE FOR BILLY CARSON'S

COMPENDIUM OF THE
EMERALD TABLETS

A Beginner's Guide

"I am so impressed with your work and your research. It was a pleasure."

– Erich Von Daniken, *Best Selling Author "Chariots Of The Gods"*
and Television Host

"Today, Billy Carson brings to our community, the Compendium of the Emerald Tablets. Finally, we are able to dive deeper into the meaning of what Thoth really intended for us to know, to explore and discover what is truly important about ourselves and the world around us."

– Jimmy Church, *JimmyChurchRadio.com,*
iHeart Radio and Coast To Coast AM

"Billy Carson is an amazing researcher that I have admired for a very long time."   – George Noory, *Coast To Coast AM*

"Billy's assimilation of scientific, metaphysical and historical concepts is mind blowing. He has an eloquent ability to relay challenging concepts in a practical way - offering each and every reader a chance to delve deeply into the scientific and spiritual mysteries of the universe."

– Bizzie Gold, *one of the world's top*
Personal Development and Wellness Experts

PRAISE FOR BILLY CARSON'S

COMPENDIUM OF THE
EMERALD TABLETS

A Beginner's Guide

"Ancient knowledge updated to a modern format. This book is a well-preserved time capsule and a must read for anyone on the path of enlightenment. D.A"

– Donny Arcade, Billboard Artist

"Billy is a thoughtful and engaging person who seeks to challenge the status quo and inform people about esoteric subjects of interest."

– Dr Tara Swart, Neuroscientist and author (M.I.T.)

"I love the fact that you travel the world and visit these ancient sites in person and do real field research. I love your work."

– Jason Martell, Television Host Ancient Aliens

COMPENDIUM OF THE
EMERALD TABLETS

A BEGINNER'S GUIDE

Billy Carson

4bidden Knowledge Inc.
Coral Springs, FL

Second Edition

ISBN: 978-0-578-47616-2
LCCN# 2019903272

Books may be purchased by contacting the publisher and author at:

4biddenknowledge Inc
934 N University Dr #417
Coral Springs, FL 33071

4biddenknowledge.com

Info@4biddenknowledge.com

Interior design and formatting by Laura C. Cantu

Cover art created by Jose M. Bethencourt Suárez

Cover art © 2019 by Billy Carson

ABOUT THE AUTHOR

Billy Carson, the founder of 4biddenknowledge.com, is a host on Deep Space, a new original streaming series by Gaia. This series explores the Secret Space Program, revealing extraordinary technologies and their potential origins. Billy Carson also serves as an expert host on Gaia's original series, Ancient Civilizations, in which a team of renowned scholars deciphers the riddles of our origins and pieces together our forgotten history documented in monuments and texts around the world. As co-founder of the United Family of Anomaly Hunters (UFAH), Billy Carson works with some of the top anomaly hunters in the world. Their mission is to provide evidence of past and present life on Earth, as well as on other celestial bodies inside our solar system. They also work to educate others about ancient technologies and their potential origins. The group is a pioneer in two new fields of science—Archeoastronomy and Astroanthropology. Billy believes that these will be offered as a college course in the not so distant future. Mr. Carson appreciates the dedication and hard work it takes to accomplish great things. Recently, Mr. Carson earned the Certificate of Science (with an emphasis on Neuroscience) at

M.I.T. Among his most notable achievements, Billy is the CEO of First Class Space Agency based in Fort Lauderdale, FL. Specifically, his space agency is involved in research and development of alternative propulsion systems and zero point energy devices.

DOCUMENTARIES AND TV SHOWS:

2017
What If (Documentary)
DocUFObia (Documentary)
Ancient Civilizations (TV Series)
Beyond Belief with George Noory (TV Series)
Life beyond Our Existence (Documentary)
Buzzsaw with Sean Stone (TV Series)

2016
The Anunnaki Series (TV Series documentary short)
Deep Space (TV Series documentary)
Baltic Sea Anomaly: The Unsolved Mystery (documentary)

2015
UFAH Favorites (Video short)

2012
Countdown to Apocalypse (TV Mini-Series documentary)

2019
UFO's: The Lost Evidence (TV Series)
World's Biggest Mysteries (TV Series)

Look for more books from Billy Carson in 2020

DEDICATION

I dedicate this book to the memory of my mother, Ingrid Carson.
She told me about the Nazca Lines and Machu Piccu in the 1970"s.
My mother believed that they may be remnants of an ancient airport.
Visiting these ancient ruins became one of the driving forces behind
my research and travels. In 2018 I fulfilled my dreams of researching
and visiting Peru where I witnessed all of its wonders. I love you Mom.
Rest In Power

WORKS BY 4BIDDENKNOWLEDGE

Listen to the 'Key Of Wisdom' by 4biddenknowledge on all music stores and streaming services.

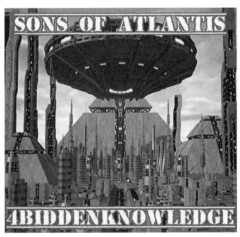

Listen to the 'Sons Of Atlantis' by 4biddenknowledge on all music stores and streaming services.

FOREWORD

All of us, no matter our background or who we are, reach a certain point in our lives when we start to see things around us a little different.

When this happens we naturally look for answers.

This not only includes those from the 'awakened' or 'new age' communities, but people from all walks of life who may have never considered our past, future or why we are here and what makes us the individuals living on this big, beautiful blue planet.

As you travel through the information from documentaries, books, lectures and the vast amount of websites on the subject of your focus, whatever it may be, you will eventually find yourself stumbling upon the Emerald Tablets of Thoth.

The moment this happens you will ask the same questions about the tablets as so many before you: 'Is this real?', 'Where are they?', 'How come I've never heard about them before?', 'Who is Thoth?' and so on... and with that your journey, that quest for knowledge, will continue.

One of the big issues today that we have with the Emerald Tablets of Thoth is the information, or lack of it, that is available for us to explore.

There have been references and translations of it that go back many centuries and it has been the centerpiece and foundation of alchemists and occult societies for it's secrets to the creation of the philosopher's stone... the true alchemical magnum opus.

So, if this is true, then why are there not volumes written about the Emerald Tablets of Thoth?

Roger Bacon, Albertus Magnus, Michael Maier, Aleister Crowley and Isaac Newton all wrote about the tablets and did their own translations- all excellent work for the time but today seems outdated by modern standards.

Over the last few hundred years, academics who were unfamiliar with hermeticism looked mainly at the direct words and didn't attempt to view and interpret the many layers and hidden meanings of the text. The pure scientific mindset instead tried to figure out the chemistry and perform the laboratory experimentation to confirm the secret of the prima materia and its transmutation.

There is a lot of information scattered around about who Thoth really was, what hermeticism is, alchemy and philosophy- but to find the real stuff is all but impossible and it's true history and meaning even harder. Putting it all together in one volume with a modern voice for our complex world has not existed, until now.

Today, Billy Carson brings to our community, the Compendium of the Emerald Tablets.

Finally, we are able to dive deeper into the meaning of what Thoth really intended for us to know, to explore and discover what is truly important about ourselves and the world around us.

There are three basic questions that we need answers:

1. Where did we come from?
2. Why are we here?
3. Where are we going?

For the enlightened, these questions are basic- but still unanswered and for those just beginning their quest they are the biggest questions of all.

This Compendium of the Emerald Tablets will help both groups find the answers they seek and finally we all have a modern, fresh take on one of the greatest mysteries of our time: The Emerald Tablets of Thoth.

Jimmy Church
Host, FADE to BLACK
September, 2018

jimmy church
host, FADE to BLACK
fill-in host, Coast to Coast AM
History Channel/A&E Networks
www.jimmychurchradio.com

www.kgraradio.com

www.coasttocoastam.com

PREFACE

Goals of The Compendium of the Emerald Tablets, A Beginner's Guide

The goal of this book is to provide you with a deep understanding of the profound and ancient knowledge that is your birthright. I will lead you on a journey that will delve into the history of the Emerald Tablets and the secret mysteries contained within these cryptic artifacts.

As we begin, it is important for you to know that The Emerald Tablets were written by an ancient being known as Thoth the Atlantean. To date, there have been two manifestations of the Emerald Tablets. First, thousands of years ago Thoth created multiple tablets of text and then concealed the location of these ancient tablets. Second, Thoth chose to incarnate as Hermes the Thrice Great. As Hermes, he carried a single Emerald Tablet.

What to Expect

In the first two chapters of this book I will provide information so you can understand and validate for yourself the role of extraterrestrials in our history. I will also offer evidence as to how Thoth the Atlantean was influential in our development as humans.

Chapters 3-17 contain the words of Thoth as translated by the American, Dr. Michael Doreal. Doreal's translation often uses stanzas—a grouping of lines used in poetry. I have kept this format to make it easy for you to recognize when the words of Thoth begin and when they end.

In each chapter, I add information and commentary to further express the meaning I find in the quotes from Thoth.

Who studied the tablets and when?

Seekers of wisdom and knowledge have studied the tablets in the Hermetic tradition up until 1925. Hermeticism is a tradition of study and spirituality based on the writings of Hermes. At that time, Thoth chose to appoint Michael Doreal, also known as Maurice, to locate and translate the original tablets.

In this text, I use Michael Doreal's study of the tablets to establish a timeline for the teachings of Thoth.

It is important to note that although my study of the Emerald Tablets will focus on the work translated by Dr. Doreal, I have taken the time to mention several other individuals, out of the many hundreds, who have studied the Emerald Tablets. Their extensive research of the Emerald

Tablets has dramatically influenced our history as human beings. In addition, I have referenced a significant number of topics, individuals, and modern-day projects that continue to influence the study of the tablets. Included throughout this entire book are links that provide additional information. These links are included to make it easier for you to do your own investigative research. I implore you to take notes and make an effort to follow through on your own individual study of the information. There are more materials and research possibilities than space allows for in this book. I hope that, as your guide, I can accelerate your awakening via the power of this information and we can expand our consciousnesses together. The Preface of Dr. Doreal's translation is a treasure chest of vital information, enabling anyone to establish the mindset needed to understand the importance of the Emerald Tablets.

TABLE OF CONTENTS

CHAPTER ONE

VALIDATING THE STUDY OF EXTRATERRESTRIAL LIFE

Documenting the Study of Alien Life

First and foremost, I would like to establish that I believe the Emerald Tablets represent the writing of an alien entity named Thoth. The written and physical evidence left on Earth, especially where the Emerald Tablets are concerned, supports that an alien force has purposely engaged with and powerfully influenced humankind.

To fully understand the implications that humans have interacted with an alien force throughout history, we must first analyze the word *alien*. Just the sound of the word, *alien*, may incite suspicion, speculation, and even fear.

How could such a small word hold such power?

Maybe because decades of negative, overly dramatic programming from television and movies have depicted aliens as monsters. These terrifying, slimy, and grotesque beings are shown to have arrived with the sole purpose of eradicating humans from the face of Earth. If this is your only understanding of the idea of aliens, then it would be perfectly natural for you to respond with fear.

Our entire universe is dualistic. Just as there are good and bad members of our societies, there are also good and bad aliens. I believe that good and evil permeates the universe. Just as there are light and dark and yin and yang, there are also good and bad. With that said, let us take a much closer look at the word *alien*.

The number one definition of alien, according to *The Merriam Webster Dictionary*, defines an alien to be a creature that comes from somewhere other than the planet Earth. The definition then highlights the word *extraterrestrial*.

Now, let us look at the definition of the word *extraterrestrial* and see what this dictionary has to say: *The Merriam Webster Dictionary* defines *extraterrestrial* as originating, existing, or occurring outside of Earth or its atmosphere.

Once you look at history and understand what it means to be an alien, you discover that life did not originate on planet Earth.

Additionally, if we reverse the role, and think of the word *alien* to be in relation with each specific planet, the word can become quite entertaining. For example, my thoughts of the word *alien* turn to humor when I realize Earthlings that traveled to the moon would be considered as aliens in relation to the moon. The Mars Project is on track to sending travelers to the Red Planet within our lifetime, to which we will arrive as aliens to Mars! If we continue our travels and encounter other lifeforms, *we* will be the alien visitors, and I would like to think that to them we will not be considered as grotesque monsters.

Do aliens exist in our solar system, in our galaxy, or in the universe?

Movies and television shows, as well as thousands of internet sites, wrestle with the idea that there is life other than humans that can travel the cosmos. Historically, this was a farfetched topic used only in discussions of the imagination.

Today, the idea of aliens is no longer so implausible or unbelievable. Mainline religious groups and entire academic departments in major universities give serious thought to the subject of aliens and extraterrestrials, two words that I use interchangeably.

How have those in authority within western civilization approached the study of life beyond planet earth?

In the most ancient of times, many great teachers and philosophers had no problem studying and hypothesizing about outer space. The arrival of the Christian church stymied beliefs regarding the study of the heavens and refused to consider the possibility that there was life outside the boundaries of Mankind. By the times of the Renaissance and the Enlightenment, most mainline academics were afraid to reveal the full extent of their discoveries in science and philosophy. Today, the findings of astroastronomers, physicists, biologists, and archaeologists are more acceptable than at any time in the last five centuries.

Almost four hundred years after the Roman Inquisition jailed Galileo in 1633 for challenging the view that the Earth was the center of the universe, the Church is preparing to celebrate his life and scientific discoveries. The church of the 21st century has taken a more modern and academic approach regarding Galileo's findings, as well as supporting the belief that there is life beyond planet Earth. The Scientific Revolution became an inescapable force, irreproachable even by the power of the Church.

Starting in 1757, the Church removed the ban on Galileo's scientific works. Yet, it was not until 1984 that the venerable Pope John Paul II verbally admitted that Galileo suffered wrongful persecution for his beliefs regarding space and beyond, using the phrase, "imprudently opposed."

Galileo was not the only famous scientist during the Renaissance seeking to understand our link to the heavens. In the 15th century, Copernicus worked his entire life establishing the heliocentric nature of our solar system, proving that the sun is the center of our solar instead of Earth. He based his studies on long-ignored documents from ancient Greece. During the course of his research, he became convinced that we were not alone in the universe. Copernicus's research finally reached publication while he lay on his deathbed, and thus was left without reproach because it would have been unthinkable to harass a dying man in the same ways Galileo had been harassed.

Catholic Influence on Our Awareness of Alien Presence

In conferences held in 2009, 2011, and 2014 the Catholic Church supported the possibility of alien life. More recently, according to the *Catholic Register* of February 23, 2018, Pope Francis was quoted during routine mass as saying, "If an expedition of Martians arrives and some of them come to us and if one of them says: 'Me, I want to be baptized!' what would happen? Who are we to close the doors?" Read more: http://www. ncregister.com/daily-news/of-space-aliens-and-the-catholic-faith.

The Vatican Observatory has been at the forefront of efforts to bridge the gap between religion and science. At the 2009 and 2011 conferences, called by Pope Benedict XVI, thirty-two scientists gathered to address "the questions of life's origins" and of whether life exists elsewhere in the universe. Meeting at the world-renowned Vatican Observatory, founded in 1582, an atmosphere of discovery, flexibility, and the possibility of being open to change could be found everywhere. Vatican Observatory scientist-clerics have generated top-notch research, collecting one of the world's most significant collection of global and other earthly data.

At the first conference in 2009, Rev. Jose Funes, director of the world-renowned Vatican Observatory, was able to present progressive results from the interdisciplinary group of astronomers, physicists, and biologists. Included among the many topics debated were life's origins and the existence of life in the universe, known as the field of astrobiology. He revealed, "Although astrobiology is an emerging field and still a developing subject, the questions of life's origins and of whether life exists elsewhere in the universe are very interesting and deserve serious consideration. These questions offer many philosophical and theological implications."

For Funes, the challenge to philosophy and theology seems to be how to find consensus within the discourse. Rev. Funes expressed to the Vatican newspaper, *L'Osservatore Romano* that one's faith in God cannot find compromise simply because one also believes in the existence of extraterrestrial life. "How can we rule out that life may have developed elsewhere? Just as there is a multitude of creatures on Earth, there could be other beings, even intelligent ones, created by God. This does not contradict our faith, because we cannot put limits on God's creative freedom." The belief that we will eventually encounter alien life is strong among most secular and church scholars today. When that life presents itself to us or when intelligent beings become aware to us, they will be considered a part of God's creation.

Read more: http://www.foxnews.com/story/2009/11/10/vatican-seeks-signs-alien-life.html.

One of the invited scientists to the conference was Chris Impey, an astronomy professor at the University of Arizona. Impey believed it to be suitable for the Vatican to hold this kind of meeting. "Both science and religion posit life as a special outcome of a vast and mostly inhospitable universe. There is a rich middle ground for dialogue between the practitioners of astrobiology and those who seek to understand the meaning of our existence in a biological universe...and whether sentient life forms exist on other worlds." With much excitement, Impey added that, "if biology is not unique to the Earth, or life elsewhere differs bio-chemically from our version, or we ever make contact with an intelligent species in the vastness of space, the implications for our self-image will be profound."

The Vastness of Our Universe and Beyond

Besides the hundreds of planets discovered outside our solar system by scientists, the European Space Agency recently announced the finding of thirty-two new planets. According to Professor Impey, we may discover alien life in measurable in years, not centuries. Planets that might sustain extraterrestrial life potentially number in the billions.

In November 2013, astronomers interpreted data from the Kepler space mission, suggesting that just within the Milky Way galaxy alone (our home galaxy), as many as forty billion Earth-sized planets may be orbiting around sun-like dwarf stars. Against that incredible number, Astronomers have discovered approximately 3,700 planets that exist in the habitable zone—the Goldilocks Zone. The Goldilocks Zone refers to those planets, like Earth, positioned "just right" from their suns for life to exist.

The task of finding the planets that exist within the Goldilocks Zone is daunting. It can be difficult to fathom that from that substantial number, life must exist. Many believe life even existed long before our scientific technology existed. Of those discovered, the closest planet within the Goldilocks zone is Proxima Centauri b, which is 4.4 light-years from Earth, which would take a mere 54,000 years using current propulsion technology. All other calculations of travel time find a basis in hypothetical systems not yet in existence.

Perhaps, life on Proxima b is calling humankind to make the trip. Perhaps, extraterrestrial life has already made the journey to Earth.

Since August 24, 2016, we have known the address of this possibly inhabitable planet, which is RA 14h 29m 43s | Dec -62° 40' 46."

There exists forty billion earth-sized planets in one galaxy! Can you believe it?

According to a news report from the Royal Astronomical Society posted on January 16, 2017, the Astrophysical Journal reports that there are approximately 2 to 10 trillion galaxies in the universe and within each galaxy, there are 200 billion stars like our sun. The obvious question left is just how many planets are there in the entire universe? Current speculation estimates four hundred eighty thousand million million million! Furthermore, with every new technological development in the field of astronomy and astrobiology, the data presents larger and larger numbers.

You might ask, "What do all of these numbers mean?"

They are markers of authenticity. Our study of the Emerald Tablets necessitates that we have a clear and profound understanding of the massive size of our universe.

Perhaps, we would be safe to declare the number of planets in our universe are unknowable. Our human minds may be too finite and limited to fully grasp the immensity of the secrets of our universe. The numbers of habitable planets are so unimaginable that there is room for every theory that has been proposed about time, space, and alien life to be validated as correct and true. There is room in the vastness of space for all of our theories to exist. Understanding the magnitude of the number of planets in our galaxy enables us to realize that the odds speak for the existence of extraterrestrial lifeforms. Simply put, it would be more unimaginable to believe that there is no alien life elsewhere in the universe than to believe that Earth is the only inhabited planet. The vast numbers of planets in the universe give credence to our understanding of ancient alien races existing over tens of thousands of years. Read more: https://phys.org/news/2017-01-universe-trillion-galaxies.html

https://www.theguardian.com/commentisfree/2017/apr/26/discovery-of-alien-life-religion-will-survive

Religion and Science

Many Christian denominations, as well as most of Catholicism, have come a long way with their strange bedfellows of science. Copernicus died before the church rejected his work, and another famous scientist did not fare so well. Giordano Bruno took the heliocentric theory a step further and wrote that our Solar System is only one of many star systems where intelligent life exists. He also indicated that there existed extraterrestrial life superior to life on Earth.

Unfortunately, the Church decided that his blasphemy necessitated punishment and burned him at the stake in 1600. Today, most of the world's religious communities avidly honor the significance of Copernicus, Bruno, and Galileo. I hope that they can rest in peace now that their ideas have found acceptance around the world.

Clerics like Funes publicly accredit scientific concepts such as the Big Bang theory as a rational explanation for the creation of the universe. The Big Bang Theory states the universe began 13.8 billion years ago after the explosion of a single, super-dense point that made up all matter. If he were alive today, Galileo would stand in proud agreement with clerics like Funes.

Aliens, Creationism, or Intelligent Design

Despite amazing strides of change and our awareness to the possibilities of Alien lifeforms, there is still some divisiveness on these matters within the Catholic Church and within other religions. Some still favor creationism or intelligent design, which makes it challenging for their supporters to accept the notion of alien life.

In addition to focusing on the scientists of the Renaissance, the Vatican sponsored another conference on evolution to mark the 150th anniversary of Charles Darwin's, *The Origin of Species*. Creationism and intelligent design theories took second billing so that attendees could focus on Darwin's main concepts of natural selection through evolution.

Pope Benedict XVI explored essential questions and worked with scientists to address areas of religious interests. His teachings, which were a crucial aspect of his papacy, reinforced the relationship between faith and reason. Though Benedict's papacy was notably supportive of traditional theology, the pontiff supported the study of extraterrestrial life. Benedict also ordered the Vatican Museums to open an exhibit on October 13, 2009 in preparation for celebrating the anniversary of Galileo's first celestial observations made in 1610.

The president of the National Institute of Astrophysics in Italy, Tommaso Maccacaro, stated at the exhibit's opening that since the sixteenth century, modern astronomy not only informs us more about space, but also contributes to an advanced realization of human consciousness.

"It was astronomical observations that let us understand that Earth (and man) doesn't have a privileged position or role in the universe," Maccacaro asserted. "I ask myself what tools will we use in the next 400 years, and I ask what revolutions of understanding they'll bring about, like resolving the mystery of our apparent cosmic solitude."

Who Believes?

The Bible makes more than one reference to unearthly visitors. "Do not forget to show hospitality to strangers, for by so doing some people have shown hospitality to angels without knowing it." Hebrews 13:2

I propose that these "Angels" are actually "Aliens."

The Christian Church is not the only religious group that has belief systems open to the existence of extraterrestrial life and otherworldly divinities. I want to stress that it is essential that you understand this. Virtually every religion that exists on this planet involves deities or a deity that claims to be "not of this world." What are the heavens after all if they are not planes of existence beyond this world?

Let's take a quick look at some of the oldest and largest religions and their emphasis upon otherworldly deities. The following numbers reflect findings by the eminent Pew Research Center:

Christianity - 2.4 billion worship Jesus. "And he said unto them, you are from beneath; I am from above: you are of this world; I am not of this world." John 8:23

Islam - 1.8 billion believe that the Prophet Muhammad was meditating in the cave of Hira by himself when the angel Gabriel (not from earth) descended (came down from above) to him and told him to "recite" the words of God, as the Prophet Muhammad was illiterate at the time.

Hinduism - 1.15 billion Hindus believe that numerous spiritual beings and deities, referred to as gods, goddesses, and devas, populate the universe and actively interact with humans and influence humankind from outside the world.

Buddhism -521 million - Buddhists refer to a varied tradition of different gods and goddesses (not of this world), but though they do not worship any major deity, they are loyal to their own beliefs. Their beliefs feature praying and chanting to Lord Buddha who provides the role model for seeking enlightenment of the divine. The modern translator of The Emerald Tablets, M. Doreal, spent many months in Tibet studying under the Dalai Lama shortly after World War I.

Mormons - 17 million - The Angel Moroni (not from earth), in Mormonism, is an angel who visited Joseph Smith on numerous occasions, beginning on September 21, 1823. According to Smith, the angel was the guardian of the golden plates that early Mormons believed were the source material for the Book of Mormon Smith had unburied from a hillside near Smith's Western New York home.

Judaism - 14 million - The Old Testament holds many accounts of otherworldly visitors. The otherworldly strangers who visited Lot, the brother of Abraham, encouraged him to leave the cities of Sodom and Gomorrah. The prophet Elijah ascended into the heavens in a chariot of fire (spaceship with retro fuel blasts). Ezekiel fills pages of his prophecy describing in detail what many consider the blueprints for a spaceship's operation. There are many, many more such examples and modern-day Judaism embraces the study of extraterrestrial life.

Famous Armenian mystic and writer George Gurdjieff searched for the source of esoteric knowledge and stated that what he found "will seem strange to many people when I say that this prehistoric Egypt was Christian many thousands of years before the birth of Christ."

He also discovered and said, "The Christian church, the Christian form of worship, was not invented by the fathers of the church in a ready-made form from Egypt, only not from the Egypt that we know but from one that we do not know. This Egypt was in the same place as the other, but it existed much earlier. Only small bits of it survived in historical times, and these bits have been preserved in secret and so well that we do not even know where they have been preserved."— P.D. Ouspensky, *In Search of the Miraculous.*

Today, the study of extraterrestrials occupies the time of secular academicians, as well as the religious. That said, not everyone is on the same page as to how or what we should call otherworldly beings. In 2014, many secularists were vehemently against NASA sending $1.1M of taxpayer dollars to the Center for Theological Inquiry, an ecumenical research institute in New Jersey, to study "the societal implications of astrobiology" and the idea of extraterrestrial life. Yet, for many aficionados of modern astrobiology and astroarchaeology, belief in aliens should be encouraged by those in and outside established religious institutions.

By researching ancient documents, such as The Emerald Tablets and studying mainstream developments in physics and astronomy, those who search for the truth will find answers. For many, it is without question that those whom we call aliens today were gods and angels in ancient times.

Carl Sagan once wrote in Cosmos, "Meanwhile, elsewhere there are an infinite number of other universes each with its own God dreaming the cosmic dream. It is said that men may not be the dreams of the Gods, but rather that the Gods are the dreams of men." Carl Sagan noted in The Cosmic Question, "Space exploration leads directly to religious and philosophical questions." Again, Carl Sagan attests that, "The origin of life on suitable planets seems built into the chemistry of the Universe."

Paul Davies explains in his book, *Are We Alone?*, "There are two principles supporting the existence of alien life. First, is the principle of abundance, stating that everything that is possible will be realized. Second, is the principle that as long as there are no obstacles to the formation of life, then life will exist."

Vanderbilt professor of Astronomy, David Weintraub, in *Religions and Extraterrestrial Life* writes, "We can quite reasonably expect that the number of known exoplanets will soon become, like the stars, almost uncountable."

http://www.bbc.com/future/story/20161215-if-we-made-contact-with-aliens-how-would-religions-react

Evolution is Serious Business

Scientists in all fields of study approach the possibility of alien life with serious consideration and have spent years researching it. For thirteen years, Maxim A. Makukov of the Fesenkov Astrophysical Institute and Vladimir I. Shcherbak from the al-Farabi Kazakh National University worked for the Human Genome Project,—a project designed to map human DNA. What the scientists found led them to believe that an extraterrestrial civilization designed humans and had a goal to preserve a message in human DNA and to seed life on various planets. The researchers concluded that, "humans are the design of a higher power with a set of arithmetic patterns and ideographic symbolic language encoded into our DNA."

The scientists went on to state that, "Ninety-seven percent of non-coding sequences in human DNA is genetic code from alien life forms." This finding was published in May of 2013 in the journal, *Icarus*, Vol. 224, in an article named, The 'Wow! signal' of the terrestrial genetic code.

Their research also states that, "a more advanced extraterrestrial civilization was engaged in creating new life and planting it on various planets. Earth is just one of them."

According to Dr. Makukov and Dr. Shcherbak, "The sudden boom in evolution experienced on Earth billions of years ago is a sign of something happening on a higher level that we are not aware of, and that mathematical code in DNA cannot explain evolution."

Dr. Makukov said, "Sooner or later, we have to accept the fact that all life on Earth carries the genetic code of our extraterrestrial cousins and that evolution is not what we think it is."

Case of Mistaken Identity

I am in a music video called "Anunnaki" by Donny Arcade that is featured on YouTube.

https://www.youtube.com/watch?v=pcE9fQCwFug&ab_channel=DonnyArcade.

In this video, you can see me using a wristwatch device to open a portal to the stars so that my crew and I can travel to Earth. In the video, we actually transport ourselves to Egypt. Imagine yourself as one of the earthlings that just happen to be there in ancient Egypt when the portal opened and we, "The Aliens," came walking through the portal. From your perspective, you would assume that we were gods or angels from another dimension or from the "Heavens."

CHAPTER TWO

HISTORY OF THE EMERALD TABLETS OF THOTH

Before we begin our examination of The Emerald Tablets, we must first address the question as to *why* there are so few certainties regarding ancient writings and texts. Most ancient texts are written on animal skins, papyrus or other perishable items. Very few writings are found on stone or baked tablets, and even those can be damaged or lost. Stone inscriptions depend on someone keeping them safe from the scrap pile of changing generations. Even fewer writings appear on precious metals.

Perishable tablets have always been susceptible to the weather and time. I should add that there are literally tens of thousands of untranslated stones in cuneiform not released in Iran and Iraq today. Who knows what messages translators will unveil in the distant future?

Inscriptions in precious metals, because of their value and rarity, are almost invariably the property and creation of kings and upper royalty personalities. Oftentimes, their contents speak only to the greatness of their owners and are in tombs, as subsequent owners have melted all others down throughout history. Yet, this brings us to discuss the difference and the constituency of the precious metal used in the creation of the ten Emerald Tablets of Thoth and the single Emerald Tablet of Hermes Trismegistus. I want to avoid confusion, but suffice it to say at this point that Thoth and Hermes are the same; but for now, I will describe how each came to be associated with their specific creations of emerald. In so doing, we will learn who they are and how important they are to our study.

Thoth ruled Egypt at a time that far outpaces our present understanding of precisely how old Egyptian civilization is. Ruling Egypt for 16,000 years from 50,000 to 36,000 BC, Thoth became the highest of highest priests of ancient Atlantis, trained by his own father the Master of Masters of pre-diluvian Atlantis. This ruling occurred after the floods that devoured the ancient civilization. Thoth ascended to Earth, where he led the development of a new civilization in the northeast corner of upper Africa, also named Khem or Egypt.

According to Dr. Doreal's translations of the tablets, there are a total of fifteen Emerald Tablets. At first, he says the tablets number ten on the first page of his Preface, but later he says they number twelve on page two of the Preface; finally, his translation ends by saying fifteen tablets exist.

The Emerald Tablets of the Atlantean Thoth laid hidden and buried under the Great Pyramid of Giza for centuries. The date of their concealment is unknown, but we do know it was sometime after Thoth left his earthly kingship over the Egyptians.

Even now, under the Great Pyramid of Giza, lies an undiscovered place of otherworldly appearance and the access point to a realm referred to as the Great Halls of Amenti. For generation upon generation, after the earthly departure of Thoth, specially appointed priests of Thoth performed as guardians to the hiding place of his domain.

Around 1200 BC, priests removed these tablets from Egypt and carried them throughout the world to all former Atlantean colonies. The further away from Egypt the priests traveled, the more new civilizations experienced religious renaissances. Finally, the priests left the tablets buried under an unmarked temple (perhaps under the pyramid of Pakal the Great) of the Mayans in Central America where Thoth became known as Quetzalcoatl and Kukulcan.

How did the Emerald Tablets find their way into the possession of the American spiritualist, Maurice Doreal?

It wasn't too long after Doreal's providential survival from the trenches of World War I that he had a revelation from Thoth. The god told him how to find the ancient Mayan pyramid housing the Tablets and to instructed him to recover the tablets for a modern translation. J.R.R. Tolkien speaks of a similar experience after his experiences in the trenches that led to his vision for the *Lord of the Rings*. "Out of chaos, comes order," says Thoth. To this dictum both Doreal and Tolkien would agree.

Doreal completed his translations of the Emerald Tablets in 1925. The tablets appear to be written in the ancient language of the Atlanteans, but Thoth gave Doreal the inspiration and guidance to complete the translation without outside assistance, much as God revealed His words to the Prophets of the Old Testament.

Thoth gave Doreal permission to retain a copy of his translations after making the arduous journey and delivering the tablets to the doorway of the Halls of Amenti. We can imagine Doreal taking a transport ship across the Atlantic in the mid-nineteen twenties bound for Egypt while concealing the glistening Emerald Tablets of Thoth the Atlantean. How he must have slipped surreptitiously into the pyramid complex under the cover of darkness, directed by the presence of Thoth to the hidden entrance. This entrance lay undisturbed for over 3300 hundred years since the guardian priests had left behind their temples for the mission of Thoth. Now 3300 years later, a new believer finds entry into the most secret of secret places, returning the gift to the ancient ones. When Doreal departed, with his back to the pyramids, Thoth sealed the entryway, which is still unknown by any living person today.

Doreal arranged the ten tablets into thirteen chapters and then supplemented the original thirteen with two more, bringing their count to fifteen. These original tablets consist of a material of transmuted emerald, meaning that, as such, they exist in a state that is unalterable, undamaged and unchanged. In this regard, they refute the law of ionization that requires all metals to change in relation to the constant alterations of positive and negative protons. Doreal was able to determine and establish their ancient consistency and durability, as they remained hidden for thousands of years. The shimmering emerald gleams with the symbols of the ancient Atlantean language, containing characters that respond to attuned thought waves, releasing the associated mental vibration in the mind of the reader. The tablets fasten together with hoops of golden-colored alloys suspended from a rod of the same material.

These most ancient tablets are the ones formed by Thoth, the god of wisdom and knowledge, and written for the spiritual enlightenment of all who will respond and receive a rarified form of consciousness as a gift from the god himself. Thoth was a God-King of Egypt for thousands of years, but when he decided to return to the Halls of Amenti, he built the Great Pyramid of Egypt to serve a two-fold function; firstly, to safeguard the Emerald Tablets and secondly, to serve as the hidden entrance to the Halls of Amenti. Thoth says that beneath The Great Pyramid stands the 'doorway' to the underworld where the Master of Masters dwells. We will learn more about the Halls of Amenti, shortly.

Upon leaving Egypt for an interlude of rest, Thoth entrusted his pyramid priests to keep the doorway and the tablets hidden until otherwise instructed. The tablets they were assigned to protect are the same Emerald Tablets that in modern time, Maurice Doreal discovered in 1925 at the instruction of Thoth. Until then, they stayed hidden for thousands of years. As I mentioned, around 1200 BC there was such unrest in Egypt, as well as throughout the entire civilized world that Thoth worried for the safety of the Tablets, yet he saw an opportunity to spread the Logos of the Tablets to Atlantean colonies throughout other, far-reaching places of the world.

Recently, a new book has become popular detailing this great collapse of civilizations, ending what historians have labeled as the Bronze Age. *"1177 BC: The Year Civilization Collapsed,"* by Eric Cline is a thorough examination of Egypt and surrounding kingdoms. From this chaos, Thoth followed his commissioned priests and during the next thousand years, his teachings manifested through him and equally through the Greek god Hermes. Both, together and separate, they epitomized the ideas of Knowledge and Wisdom, among other lesser attributes. There is a difference of opinion regarding how Hermes appears with the nomer, "the Thrice-Great." However, from this tradition evolves a body of literature called the *Hermetic Corpus*. In addition to teaching knowledge, wisdom, and immortality, it also provides instruction in alchemy, astrology, and magic. Out of this tradition, there emerges by the fifth century AD a single Emerald Tablet with fourteen sayings. This is referred to in literature From ancient times up to the present; literature credits these teachings to Thoth and Hermes, as they are the same. Translating this tablet has proven to be challenging as translators no longer have access to the original, which disappeared in the first millennium AD. What remained were various translations by high-ranking priests and scholars within the Hermetic tradition. Therefore, modern translations are often the translations of translations. Keep in mind; all references to the Emerald Tablet of Hermes Trismegistus refer to a single tablet made of emerald with the same impenetrable consistency as the original Emerald Tablets. I think this might be confusing for some; therefore, it will be important to illustrate the brevity of the teachings on the single tablet of Hermes.

For several millennia, there has been a historical and academic appreciation of the single Emerald Tablet of Hermes. The Hermes text, written in Thoth's Atlantean language and modern images and representations of The Emerald Tablets/Tablet often show one tablet, signifying the Hermes tablet. The original and expanded, multiple tablet version is the focus of this book. Our focus is on the Emerald Tablets of Thoth the Atlantean, translated by Dr. Michael (also Maurice) Doreal in 1925 and can be found online here: https://www.bibliotecapleyades.net/thot/esp_thot_1.htm.

Also, the Brotherhood Of The White Temple (the Institute of ancient studies founded by Dr. Doreal), is still functioning today and you can find copies of Dr. Doreal's translation at their website: https://brotherhoodofthewhitetemple.com

Now, let me provide you with the complete translation of the Emerald Tablet of Hermes Trismegistus used by scholars since the Egyptian dispersion until modern times (all on one page). The following translation comes from Sir Isaac Newton:

1.   Tis true without error, certain & most true.

2. That which is below is like that which is above & that which is above is like that which is below to do the miracles of one only thing.

3. And as all things have been & arose from one by the mediation of one: so all things have their birth from this one thing by adaptation.

4. The Sun is its father, the moon its mother, the wind hath carried it in its belly, the earth is its nurse.

5. The father of all perfection in the whole world is here.

6. Its force or power is entire if it be converted into earth.

7. Separate thou the earth from the fire, the subtle from the gross sweetly with great industry.

8. It ascends from the earth to the heaven & again it descends to the earth & receives the force of things superior & inferior.

9. By this means you shall have the glory of the whole world

10. & thereby all obscurity shall fly from you.

11. Its force is above all force. For it vanquishes every subtle thing & penetrates every solid thing.

12. So was the world created.

13. From this are & do come admirable adaptations whereof the means (or process) is here in this. Hence I am called Hermes Trismegistus, having the three parts of the philosophy of the whole world.

14. That which I have said of the operation of the Sun is accomplished & ended.

You can do further research on Newton's commentaries on the Tablets by following this link: https://ashleycowie.com/new-blog/sir-isaac-newton-and-the-emerald-tablet

The words of the single Tablet are valuable in their own right, but differ radically from the Tablets translated by Doreal in 1925, which occupy about 90 pages in standard verse form, which is quite a difference.

A rendering of The Hermes Trismegistus Emerald Tablet

We will now look briefly at some references to space travel, alien encounters, and other such narratives of historical figures in order to provide context.

Egyptian Texts

Certain hieroglyphic texts state that one chapter of *The Book of the Master of the Hidden Places* was still in existence during the reign of Hesep-ti, about 4266 BC; Egyptologists deemed it as the most ancient documentation of any kind known in the world. Consequently, *The Book of the Dead* is known as the first secret manual of initiation. Among its teaching, there are descriptions of procedures and passwords that have two specific levels of meaning, one spiritual and the other physical. The 'Hidden Places' mentioned in the aforementioned book are in reference to underground chambers at the Giza complex (Halls of Amenti). *The Book of the Dead* carries some unusual narratives, with a curious reference to 'those who live among the stars.' Another passage mentions a specific knowledge that enabled those in its possession to 'reach the vault of the sky.'

The Writers of the Bible and Ancient Sumer

Thoth had many names over the eons. In Sumeria, he was Ningishzida son of Enki. Ancient Sumerian clay cylinder seals record the story of two special emissaries 'clothed like birds, with wings for garments.' In the fragments of some Chaldean tablets found in 1870 is inscribed the Babylonian Legend of Creation wherein the first column of what is called the Cutha Tablet, a description was given of seven particular human beings 'with the faces of ravens' that came and instructed the local inhabitants with new knowledge.

Without The Great Pyramid and the mysterious *The Book of the Dead* by Thoth, there would be no Bible today, simply because the very essence of the hidden information evolved at the Great Pyramid.

The Old Testament prophet Ezra's secret message decoded by Sir Francis Bacon revealed that the 'King's Temple' was the famous Temple of Solomon. The Hall of Pillars in Solomon's Temple consisted of seven columns, a symbol taken from the earlier description of a Hall of Pillars in *The Book of the Dead*. Solomon's Temple was full of symbols to hide the fact that Ezra was talking secretly about a real Temple at Giza.

The Book of the Dead recorded that the god Thoth was designer and builder of the Great Pyramid. These words were carved into stone at the very dawn of civilization on planet Earth. Elements of that same story also appear in pyramid texts that date to around 2450 BC and presented in a context that suggested their ancient age.

Jesus is a special subject that we will focus upon more than once throughout the book. The flight into Egypt is a biblical event described in Matthew 2:13-23. The Magi learned that King Herod intended to murder the infants within that area, and soon after Joseph saw an angel in a dream, which told him to flee to Egypt with Mary and his infant son, Jesus.

The Great Pyramid of Egypt has been and still is a temple of initiation into the mysteries. Gnostic texts such as, *The First Apocalypse of James,* were likely banned because of their different understanding of Jesus' importance. "They understood Jesus much more in terms of being a revealer of human wisdom," explains Brent Landau, a religious studies lecturer at the University of Texas at Austin, who presented the findings at the Society of Biblical Literature Annual Meeting in Boston in November 2017. *The First Apocalypse of James* Manuscript is from the Nag Hammadi Library/Oxford University.

Coptic Church in Old Cairo – Living quarters of Jesus – Billy Carson

Many believe *The Emerald Tablets of Thoth* are the source material for the teachings of Jesus in the New Testament. If you read the Apocrypha texts, you will find out that Jesus was a student of the Egyptian Mysteries and he taught reincarnation and meditation. I know this to be true because on my last trip to Cairo I visited the Coptic Church where Jesus and his mother lived while there. They lived under the church in the basement. The Council of Nicaea in 325 AD omitted that information from the canonized bible. I have included photos that I took in May 2014 of the living place of Jesus and his mother in Egypt. It is still kept as a memorial until now. This biblical story of the birth of Jesus is about the SUN and planetary alignments. The real person named Yeshua (Jesus) is actually Thoth or the son of Thoth in my personal opinion. More recently, the biggest discovery is a writing called the gospel of Jesus Wife. Yes, he was married and had children. His bloodline still walks the earth to this very day. Behind me are photos that I took in May 2014 of the living place of Jesus and his mother in Egypt. A well-known story in the east recounts that Jesus was a student of the Mystery Schools and upon leaving there he traveled to Tibet and India where he learned energetic healing and meditation.

The Queen of Sheba

According to D.J. Conway in Crystal Enchantment, the Queen of Sheba knew about the original Emerald Tablet of Thoth. The Queen of Sheba is a figure first mentioned in the Hebrew Bible. She introduced Solomon to the great mines of Africa, including extensive emerald mines. Their story has been elaborated and expanded over the many years by Jewish, Islamic, and Ethiopian cultures, and has become one of the most popular legends in the ancient near east.

https://www.pbs.org/mythsandheroes/myths_four_sheba.html

Pythagoras

Followers of Pythagoras accepted as law any decisions communicated by him, and honored him as an emissary from Zeus. Pythagoras is famous for his teaching of the 'transmigration of souls,' which states that "every soul is immortal and, upon death, enters into a new body (reincarnation)." He is also credited with developing 'musica universalis,' which state that "the planets move according to mathematical equations, and thus, resonate to produce an inaudible symphony of music." Pythagoras' philosophies of the solar system profoundly influenced Plato, Alexander of Tyana,

Copernicus, and Sir Isaac Newton

In the ancient world, there was widespread belief in the existence of exalted knowledge that was accessible only to initiated people, knowledge that, by definition, conveyed a sense of awe. The fundamental nature of their illuminated teaching deals with a transcendent realm. The great teachers of history, such as Socrates, Pythagoras, Aristotle, Virgil, Homer, Apollonius of Tyana were all initiates in the ancient Sacred Mysteries; they knew the Secret knowledge. Other initiates include Plato, Plutarch, Celsus, Clement of Alexandria, Plotinus, Porphyry and on and on making an almost inexhaustible list. Both Plotinus and Plato explained the 'divine visions of the Mysteries' as a secret science sought by many but known only to a few. Ancient Egyptian priests often referred to a 'Secret Science' known to them; so formidable was its power they taught it to no one who had not been firstly prepared, tested and accepted. https://plato.stanford.edu/entries/pythagoreanism/

Manetho and Early Church Fathers

Manetho was an Egyptian priest who lived during the early Third Century BC and authored the History of Egypt, a significant source detailing Egypt's ancient rulers. According to Manetho, Thoth wrote 36,525 books. An ancient Egyptian story tells how The Book of Thoth first appeared. According to Thoth himself, the book contains the secrets as to how humans may perceive the gods. Such knowledge was not available to the average human and, subsequently, hidden from humankind for hundreds of years at a time. It was dangerous to attempt to use the book without Thoth's permission. On one such occasion, safeguarded by serpents, sealed in a golden box and hidden at the bottom of the Nile River, Prince Neferkaptah recovered it. Thoth's wrath was quick and unyielding as he drove the prince to suicide and wiped out his entire family. For centuries, the book lay hidden in Neferkaptah tomb. *The Book of Thoth* lay hidden for a thousand years until uncovered by the Chief Priest of Memphis in the 11th century BC. This special priest was extremely interested in magic, alchemy, and other ancient manuscripts of wisdom. How he discovered the ancient Prince's tomb is unknown, but upon finding it, *The Book of Thoth* revealed itself. Khaemweset was not only the Chief Priest, but he was also the Crown Prince of Ramses the Great, but died before he was able to assume the throne. Upon attempting to interpret the ancient book, the ghost of Neferkaptah appears to humiliate him before Ramses, pressuring the Crown Prince to return the book to the tomb and seal it away until Thoth decides upon its future use by humanity. https://www.jstor.org/stable/20190475

Titus Flavius Clemens of the Second Century AD is the early church's primary source to understanding ancient Egyptian manuscripts. Prior to becoming a Christian, Clemens was the greatest scholar of his time. He excelled in translating ancient texts from Egypt and Greece. He confirms in his book the Miscellanies that the teachings of the ancients, including the Book of Thoth and that of Hermes Trismegistus, whom we know was Thoth incarnate, heavily influences Christianity. In manuscript fragments, such as *The Hypotheses*, Clemens detailed late in his life an esoteric understanding of some facets of the Ascension of Man. In addition, he seems to reflect the Seventh Tablet found in Doreal's translation of The Emerald Tablets. Clemens teaches that the Universe unfolds as the Face of God, followed by Seven Lords who are higher than all other gods, demigods, angels or humans. Clemens warned future scholars of Christianity that only the most capable of humans could be trusted with these mysteries. The significance of this fact increases, when we understand that Clemens' pupils in bulk become the Church Fathers of Christianity. http://www.earlychurch.com/clement.php

Saint Thomas Aquinas

The Book of Causes, written by Saint Thomas Aquinas in the 13th century AD, translates the Hermetic Emerald Tablet from a 9th century AD, unknown Arabian source, which Aquinas is able to prove was taken from Proclus' *Elements of Theology* (sometime in the 5th century AD)

"all things are part of a single continuous emanation of power from the One." Thomas of Aquinas was a Catholic priest and Doctor of the Church whose works would influence most great thinkers of from the middle ages up to present times. https://www.iep.utm.edu/aquinas/

Sir Isaac Newton

One of the most influential scientists of all time, Sir Isaac Newton was an English mathematician, theologian, astronomer, author and physicist. He was known as a key player who revolutionized science. His book, *Mathematical Principles of Natural Philosophy,* which was published in 1687, was paramount in laying the foundations of classical mechanics. Newton's Principia formulated the laws of motion and universal gravitation that dominated scientists' view of the physical universe for the next three centuries. Newton removed the last doubts about the validity of the heliocentric model of the Solar System and demonstrated that the motions of objects on Earth and of celestial bodies rest on the same principles. https://plato.stanford.edu/entries/newton-principia/

Philip of Tripoli

Philip of Tripoli translated The Hermetic Emerald Tablet in the 13th c. AD. Originally, Philip had translated the lost Greek manuscript, *The Secret Book of Secrets.* This is important because the lost manuscript supposedly came from Aristotle as a treatise on life to his most famous pupil, Alexander the Great in 330 BC. Philip spent decades of his life pouring over The Secret Book of Secrets's contents to reveal not only the teachings of Hermes Trismegistus, but also other ancient Egyptian and Greek teachings regarding the secret of wisdom as taught by Thoth the Atlantean. His abridged version was available to readers of the High Middle Ages and became the most sought after text in the western world. Inherent in its teachings, Roger Bacon found the truth of wisdom and life as are fundamental to the wisdom of Thoth. https://www.iep.utm.edu/bacon-ro/

Roger Bacon

Roger Bacon is one of the earliest European advocates of the modern scientific method inspired by Aristotle. Bacon's major work, the *Opus Majus,* was sent to Pope Clement IV in Rome in 1267 upon the pope's request. Thus, because of the high-level acceptance of his works, the ideologies of the Hermetic Emerald Tablet filtered voluminously throughout the halls of Europe's intelligentsia. https://www.iep.utm.edu/bacon-ro/

Sir Francis Bacon

Sir Francis believed he had discovered the "true extent of subterranean chambers below the sands of the Pyramid Plateau at Giza." The number 7 was the most important number in religious literature, and that may have originated with the mysterious layout in the *Book of Thoth*. The hidden knowledge in Thoth's book reveals itself in later chapters and involves another of Bacon's works, *The Wisdom of the Ancients*. That book, published in 1619, was an allegorical interpretation of hidden truths contained in ancient myths. Sir Francis Bacon learned many truths from his initiation into the Knights Templar and coded much of his understanding using the cipher 33. Bacon's favorite cipher system he called 'The Capital Initial Code. That code spells out the following: TEMPLE OF SOLOMON HIDDEN UNDER PYRAMID. He also found in 33 consecutive letters) the words, JESUS CHRIST, INITIATION, GREAT PYRAMID. https://www.philosophybasics.com/philosophers_ bacon_francis.html

Professor Carl Jung

Swiss psychiatrist and psychotherapist named Carl Gustav Jung who founded analytical psychology, took inspiration from the Emerald Tablets to write a book called *Seven Sermons To The Dead*. The Emerald Tablet is the only piece of non-Greek Hermetica to attract worldwide attention because it teaches a person how to set their level of consciousness to a new degree. Jung was a pupil of Sigmund Freud, but soon broke away from his teacher's philosophies. Instead, Jung devoted much research to the development and intricacies of human consciousness. Jung's most famous study was of the Collective Unconscious, a term he coined. https://www.psychologistworld.com/ cognitive/carl-jung-analytical-psychology

More about Pyramids

The Great Pyramid – Billy Carson

The ancient Greek historian Herodotus, believed that Khufu (aka Cheops) enslaved his people to build his pyramid. Keep in mind that the proposed method of building the pyramid was by using mud ramps. The only problem with this theory is the mass of the ramps needed would actually be far greater than the mass of the pyramid itself. This is why we need to pay close attention to the Emerald Tablets, because this 36,000-year-old text states the Thoth built the Great Pyramid, which would backdate the age of the pyramid considerably. Once you go back in time two full processional periods of the equinox, you then arrive at a time when the Sphinx aligns with the constellation Leo. Now the apparent weathering of the Sphinx and its erosion make sense. You can further explore this research by reading Graham Hancock's, *The Mystery of the Sphinx*. The geologist Robert Schoch has done an incredible amount of research and inspection of the Great Pyramid and the Sphinx. His work has been the focal point of several documentaries, which underline the significance of his arguments which establish the age of the pyramids to be much older than modern Egyptologists are willing to accept. https://www.robertschoch.com/sphinx.html

Billy Carson

One of the biggest falsehoods about the Aztecs and Mayans is that they were responsible for building the city and pyramids at Teotihuacan and Chichen-Itza, as well as the surrounding areas. My trip to Teotihuacan in Oct of 2016 confirmed this when my archeologist guide said that neither the Mayans nor the Aztecs founded or built Teotihuacan. The city complex was already there when they arrived. They merely inherited what they attributed to being the buildings, temples, and pyramids of the gods.

Once you begin to research the historical timeline of settlements and trade in that region, you start to see how our understanding of the architecture is severely misguided. Teotihuacan's builders remain an absolute mystery. The empire of the Aztecs began almost a thousand years after Teotihuacan had become desolate.

The Nahuatl-speaking Aztecs gave the city its name, meaning "the city of the gods." Some believe this city flourished between 1000 BC and 550 AD. The main cities of the Mayan, who were much more ancient (2600 BC), were 700 to 1000 miles away and would have had little reason to interact with another culture over mountains and treacherous jungles. Compare these timelines with Egyptian timelines.

https://knowledgenuts.com/.../the-difference-between-the-aztec-maya-inca-and-olmec/
Might this have been the hiding place for the Emerald Tablets discovered by Doreal in 1925? https://www.khanacademy.org/humanities/art-americas/.../a/palenque-classic-period

Comparison of a motherboard to the Mayan pyramids.

Archaeologist believe that the advanced design of Teotihuacan suggests that ancient builders had knowledge, not only of architecture, but also of complex mathematical and astronomical sciences.

The layout of the three main pyramids in Teotihuacan resemble a modern-day circuit board with processors, and the underground channels that link the pyramid city are full of electrical insulators. Two large processor chips can be seen as the Sun Pyramid and the Moon Pyramid. This city was clearly a large electrical device.

Although this level of detail is unique to Teotihuacan and many other details come into clearer focus from the sky, researchers have also found numerous and remarkable similarities to the Great Pyramids of Egypt. We know that the placement of these ancient monuments was not random, but positioned according to mathematical, geometrical, and geographical influence.

Is it possible that in the city layout of Teotihuacan a hidden Pyramid code is waiting for exposure? Hundreds of unknown metal objects lay buried there and the pyramid complex aligns with the Orion Belt just like the pyramids at Giza, as well as those in China. The base of the Pyramid of the Sun is the same size as the base at the Great Pyramid in Egypt. The height of the Pyramid of the Sun is exactly fifty percent of the height of the Great Pyramid in Egypt, with both standing on top of aquifers. https://apps.facebook.com/4biddenKnowledge/photos/a.10 7419456099725/424154464426221/?type=3&theater

Also see:

https://www.nationalgeographic.com/archaeology-and-history/.../teotihuacan/

https://enjoyandwatch.press/electrical-material-found-in-the-pyramids/

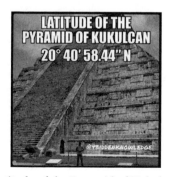

Latitude of the Pyramid of Kukulcan

"EYE AM" standing at the base of the Pyramid of Kukulcan (AKA Quetzalcoatl AKA THOTH) at Chichen-Itza in the Yucatan Peninsula. Here are some interesting facts!

Latitude of the pyramid of Kukulcan:

20° 40' 58.44" N, now multiply.

20 x 40 x 58.44 = 46752

This pyramid is a precise calendar (it has 91 steps on each of 4 sides plus platform on top: 4×91 +1 = 365).

The calendar connection is also confirmed by the pyramid's orientation marking equinoxes and solstices.

The pyramid has 4 sides with 4 staircases dividing each side into 2 sections (in total 8 sections).

Using these numbers and accurate value for one year to equal 365.25, the pyramid "number" will perfectly relate its latitude:

365.25 x 4 x4 x 8 = 46752

Billy Carson – 1998 – Chichen-Itza – Yucatan

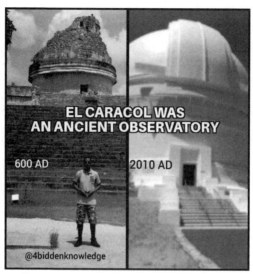

Billy Carson – 2018– Chichen-Itza – Yucatan

"EYE AM" standing in front of El Caracol, which is an ancient observatory built by Kukulcan (AKA Thoth) and used much later by the Mayans. You can clearly see the resemblance of what we call a "Modern Observatory." The official date of the construction given as 600 AD is most likely incorrect. The structure probably dates back much farther in time. El Caracol aligns with the motions of Venus. The Maya assigned Venus remarkable significance. This bright planet stands in as the sun's twin and also serves as a god of war. Mayan leaders scheduled suitable times for their raids according to the position of Venus as it drifted through the heavens. The position of Venus was so important, that the Maya built El Caracol's grand staircase to perfectly match Venus's most northerly position in the sky. The staircase faces 27.5 degrees north of west, which is out of line with all the other buildings at the site. Additionally, the other buildings form a diagonal at the northeast and southwest corners which aligns with the winter solstice sunset and the summer solstice sunset. Providing this kind of detailed information that is not easily found is why they call me #4biddenKnowledge.

Rocket man comparisions

Lord Pakal, the 'Rocket man' from the past. This image clearly resembles, with its modern day rocket interior, an exact match with the image that was revealed by archaeologist Alberto Ruz Lhuillier in 1952. Today, scholars recognize that globally advanced civilizations did exist in the ancient past. The Atlanteans were already building pyramids and temples around the world. Pakal the Great's marvelous city of pyramids flourished in the seventh century AD and still stands as one of the greatest civilizations of the Americas.

https://www.ancient-origins.net

Storming of the Teocalli by Cortez and His Troops," 1848, painting by Emanuel Leutze

After the conquest of the Central and South American civilizations by the Spaniards, the cities were abandoned, and the treasures of the temples forgotten.

Water and Emeralds

Physicists have managed to 'dissolve' water in an emerald. It shouldn't be possible. Several Russian research teams and other teams from European countries, along with Scientists from MIPT, confined water molecules within nanocages in a beryl crystal and documented the phenomenon of water molecular dipoles becoming ordered. "In solid-state physics, the notion of ferroelectricity refers to the property of a material whose electric dipole moments, while cooling, align themselves in an ordered pattern. Our team has succeeded in placing water molecules under conditions allowing us to obtain the first-ever reliable observations of the alignment of molecular dipoles of water. The electric fields, generated by nano-confined water, could play a vital role in various phenomena studied in biology, chemistry, geology, and meteorology, or even in the formation of the planets of our Solar System. In fact, many computer calculations and simulations do predict the alignment of water molecular dipoles, provided that hydrogen bonds are somehow diverted to target the artificially introduced surfaces or cavities such as carbon nanotubes or two-dimensional metal substrates." The Moscow Institute of Physics and Technology have published the result of their work in Nature Communications. http://www.geologyin.com/2016/10/scientists-dissolve-water-in-emerald.html#LERrdsvqBDpa4rWB.99

Doreal's Preface

Doreal's Preface needs recalling before we look at the actual texts of The Emerald Tablets. Written in 1925, the Preface outlines for students of the Tablets his Philosophy of how he approaches the translation and care of the Tablets. Doreal writes:

In the following pages, I will reveal some of the mysteries which as yet have only been touched upon lightly either by myself or other teachers or students of truth.

Man's search for understanding of the laws which regulate his life has been unending, yet always just beyond the veil which shields the higher planes from material man's vision the truth has existed, ready to be assimilated by those who enlarge their vision by turning inward, not outward, in their search.

In the silence of material senses lies the key to the unveiling of wisdom. He who talks does not know; he who knows does not talk. The highest knowledge is unutterable, for it exists as an entity in lanes, which transcend all material words or symbols.

All symbols are but keys to doors leading to truths, and many times the door is not opened because the key seems so great that the things which are beyond it are not visible. If we can understand that all keys, all material symbols are manifestations, are but extensions of a great law and truth, we will begin to develop the vision, which will enable us to penetrate beyond the veil.

All things in all universes move according to law and the law, which regulates the movement of the planets is no more immutable than the law which regulates the material expressions of man.

One of the greatest of all Cosmic Laws is that which is responsible for the formation of man as a material being. The great aim of the mystery schools of all ages has been to reveal the workings of the Law, which connect man the material and man the spiritual. The connecting link between the material man and the spiritual man is the intellectual man, for the mind partakes of both the material and immaterial qualities. The aspirant for higher knowledge must develop the intellectual side of his nature and so strengthen his will that is able to concentrate all powers of his being on and in the plane, he desires.

The great search for light, life and love only begins on the material plane. Carried to its ultimate, its final goal is complete oneness with the universal consciousness. The foundation in the material is the first step; then comes the higher goal of spiritual attainment.

In the following pages, I will give an interpretation of the Emerald Tablets and their secret, hidden, and esoteric meanings. Concealed in the words of Thoth are many meanings that do not appear on the surface. Light of knowledge brought to bear upon the Tablets will open many new fields for thought.

'Read and be wise,' but only if the light of your own consciousness awakens the deep-seated understanding which is an inherent quality of the soul.

WOW!!! DEEP!!!

The translator of the Emerald Tablets, who was connected with the Great White Lodge and worked his way through the pyramid priesthood, was given instruction to recover and return the ancient tablets to the Great Pyramid.

The quote below comes from the Preface and Introduction of *The Emerald Tablets of Thoth*, translated by Michael Doreal:

This, after adventures which need not be detailed here, was accomplished. Before returning them, he was permitted to translate and retain a copy of the wisdom engraved on the tablets.

This was done in 1925 and only now has permission been given for part to be published. It is expected that many will scoff. Yet the true student will read between the lines and gain wisdom.

If the light is in you, the light which is engraved in these tablets will respond.

Now, a word as to the material aspect of the tablets. They consist of twelve tablets of emerald green, formed from a substance created through alchemical transmutation. (Transmutation is the changing of one element into another by radioactive decay, nuclear bombardment, or similar processes.) They are imperishable, resistant to all elements and substances. In effect, the atomic and cellular structure is fixed, no change ever taking place.

In this respect, they violate the material law of ionization. Upon them are engraved characters in the ancient Atlantean language: characters which respond to attuned thought waves, releasing the associated mental vibration in the mind of the reader.

The tablets are fastened together with hoops of golden-colored alloy suspended from a rod of the same material. So much for the material appearance.

The wisdom contained therein is the foundation of the ancient mysteries. And for the seeds with open eyes and mind, his wisdom shall be increased a hundredfold.

http://www.crystalinks.com/emerald.html

CHAPTER THREE

THE HISTORY OF THOTH, THE ATLANTEAN

Emerald Tablet One

Thoth on an emerald tablet

In this chapter, I will establish the true source of the teachings of Jesus. It appears that most of his biblical teachings and statements come directly from the Emerald Tablets. This also points to the possibility that Jesus may be Thoth or the son of Thoth.

The 'Lost Labyrinth of Egypt' is without a doubt one of those incredible ancient sites that are a lost jewel to today's history. Image Credit: www. ancient-code.com

The fourth century Greek Historian, Herodotus records one of history's first tour guides to the ancient, and to the Greeks, mysterious Egypt. "This I have actually seen, a work beyond words. For if anyone put together the buildings of the Greeks and display of their labours, they would seem lesser in both effort and expense to this labyrinth...Even the pyramids are beyond words, and each was equal to many and mighty works of the Greeks. Yet the labyrinth surpasses even the pyramids." Herodotus, *Histories*, Book, II, 148.

AND THOTH SAID

I, THOTH, the Atlantean, master of mysteries,
keeper of records, mighty king, magician,
living from generation to generation,
being about to pass into the halls of Amenti.

These records of the mighty wisdom of Great Atlantis.
set down for the guidance of
those that are to come after,
In the great city of Keor on the island of Undal,
in a time far past, I began this incarnation.

In these passages we can see already that the tone is set for reincarnation and regeneration. Very similar to this Biblical statement In II Corinthians 5:2-7 "We grow weary in our present bodies, and we long to put on our heavenly bodies like new clothing. For we will put on heavenly bodies;

we will not be spirits without bodies. While we live in these earthly bodies, we groan and sigh, but it's not that we want to die and get rid of these bodies that clothe us. Rather, we want to put on our new bodies so that these dying bodies will be swallowed up by life. God himself has prepared us for this, and as a guarantee he has given us his Holy Spirit. So we are always confident, even though we know that as long as we live in these bodies we are not at home with the Lord. For we live by believing and not by seeing."

AND THOTH SAID

Not as the little men of the present age did
the mighty ones of Atlantis live and die,
but rather from aeon to aeon did they renew
their life in the Halls of Amenti where the river of life
flows eternally onward.

Jesus says in the New Testament book of John 7:38 "He that believes in me, out of his being shall flow rivers of living water."

AND THOTH SAID

A hundred times ten
have I descended the dark way that led into light,
and as many times have I ascended from the
darkness into the light my strength and power renewed.
Now for a time I descend,
and the men of Khem
shall know me no more.

Understand here that "men of Khem" refers to the people of Egypt. Yet, notice that we get our word *alchemy* from this Egyptian name. There are other interesting statements made by the writer Thoth. He says that he has descended into the Halls of Amenti where there is a regeneration chamber. Certainly, we can understand the concept of cellular regeneration. He says he has spent a total of 10,000 years (100x10), regenerating his avatar over the course of many eons. Thoth also references the river of life, stating, "I began this incarnation from aeon to aeon where the river of life flows eternally onward." Remember how Jesus makes the same reference in John 7:38. "Whoever believes in me, as Scripture has said, rivers of living water will flow from within them." Keep in mind, the Emerald Tablets predate the Bible by 36,000 years. Genesis 2:10-14, which mentions "river of life into four heads" and juxtaposes with Stedman's Medical Dictionary the reference of a river of cerebrospinal fluid into four chambers of the brain.

Protection: CSF

- **brain contains fluid-filled chambers = Ventricles**
  - **2 lateral ventricles, 1 third ventricle, 1 fourth ventricle**
  - connects to the **central canal** which runs into the spinal canal
  - These chambers contain *cerebrospinal fluid*
  - made by specialized cells in the ventricles– *choroid plexus (ependymal cells)*

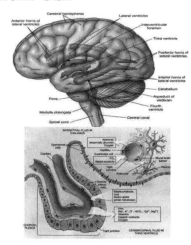

Four Chambers Of The Human Brain – Image Credit – Protection CSF
slideplayer.com

The more we read the Emerald Tablets, we realize more readily the connection between Thoth and Jesus. I believe it is very possible that they are one in the same.

AND THOTH SAID

But in a time yet unborn will I rise again,
mighty and potent, requiring an accounting
of those left behind me.

Another interesting statement made by Thoth many thousands of years before Jesus tells his disciples that he will rise again in Mark 9:31.

AND THOTH SAID

Then beware, O men of Khem,

if ye have falsely betrayed my teaching,
for I shall cast ye down from your high estate
into the darkness of the caves from whence ye came.

Betray not my secrets
to the men of the North
or the men of the South
lest my curse fall upon ye.
Remember and heed my words,
for surely will I return again
and require of thee that which ye guard.
Aye, even from beyond time and
from beyond death will I return, rewarding or punishing
as ye have requited your trust.

In the biblical text of John 14:20 Jesus declares to his followers, "I go away and come again unto you. Tell no one the son of man be risen again."

Thoth says, "For surely I will come again...betray not my secrets."

The Bible also teaches of a judgement day. Everyone, the still living and the resurrected dead, will face God's judgment. Even those who profess Christianity will find judgment through the deeds they have done in life, according to Matthew 7:21-23 and II Corinthians 5:10. Those who have lived righteous lives will be granted eternal life; those who have lived evil lives will be condemned to eternal punishment. This record appears in several biblical passages, including Matthew 5:29-30, 25:31-46, and Mark 9:43-48. Again, these statements are very reminiscent of the same things stated by Thoth over 36,000 years ago.

Did Jesus Christ (sometimes referred to as Yeshua) teach reincarnation?

The answer may shock you.

Yes! Jesus *did* teach reincarnation!

Additionally, reincarnation appears in the Old Testament. Read the last words of the Old Testament in the Book of Malachi: "Behold, I will send you Elijah the prophet before the coming of the great and dreadful day of the Lord. And he shall turn the heart of the fathers to the children, and the heart of the children to their fathers, lest I come and smite the earth with a curse." (Malachi 4:5-6). Here is God speaking through Malachi.

He was a famous prophet often quoted by great leaders throughout history, including U.S. presidents (Donald Trump), and actually saying that Elijah is going to come again.

Now, we find Jesus making the same statement. In the Book of Matthew Jesus says, "Among them that are born of women there hath not risen a greater than John the Baptist: notwithstanding he that is least in the kingdom of heaven is greater than he." Matthew 11:11.

Then he says, "And if ye will receive it, this is Elias, which was for to come," Matthew 11:14, meaning his coming was prophesied. Therefore, Jesus said, "He came. He was beheaded. They did with him what they would. And so they will do to me."

Scriptures concerning the coming again of Elijah flow so prominently throughout the Bible that anyone can accept the fact that they appear within the context of an already established canon. If reincarnation is so important, why is it not taught in the West? Some religious leaders have attempted to control people using fear tactics by saying, "You know, if you don't do what I tell you to do, you're going to go to hell." I think the early Church Fathers feared that if people understood reincarnation, they wouldn't go to church but would just wave a hand at the father and say, "Well, I'll go in my next life."

The Apostle Paul teaches the Corinthians, "For we know that when this earthly tent we live in is taken down (that is, when we die and leave this earthly body), we will have a house in heaven, an eternal body made for us by God himself and not by human hands. We grow weary in our present bodies, and we long to put on our heavenly bodies like new clothing. For we will put on heavenly bodies; we will not be spirits without bodies. While we live in these earthly bodies, we groan and sigh, but it's not that we want to die and get rid of these bodies that clothe us. Rather, we want to put on our new bodies so that these dying bodies will be swallowed up by life." II Corinthians 5:1ff.

The idea that John had been Elias (or Elijah) and that the prophets could relive again on Earth is to be found in many passages of the New Testament but is most notably quoted in Matthew 16: 13-17, Luke 9: 7-9, and Matthew 17: 10-13. If this is an erroneous belief, Jesus would have combated it as he did many others. But from this he gave complete sanction and authority by making it a basic principle and necessary condition by adding, "No one may reach the Kingdom of God if he is not born again," in John 3:3. Furthermore, insisting such when he added in John 3:7, "Do not be surprised when I say it is necessary to be born again."

In John Chapter 4, Jesus' words, "If man is not born again of water and of Spirit" are interpreted in the sense of regeneration by means of the water of Baptism. However, in the original text it was said, "not born of water and of Spirit," whereas, in some translations the words "of Spirit" have been substituted by "Holy Spirit," which does not correspond to the original meaning.

So it has always been a question of control by religious authority. If the people know too much, they will have too much power and too much independence. This is what disturbs those who try to hold the secrets of the kingdom while also trying to control people by that knowledge.

"If man is not born again of water and of Spirit"

To enable the real meaning of the above quote to be reached, it is also necessary to pay attention to the significance of the word *water,* which is not used here in its usual sense. The knowledge of physics was imperfect in ancient times, as many believed that the Earth had risen out of the water. Therefore, water is the exclusive primitive generating substance as taught in the Old Testament book of Genesis. "...the Spirit of God moved upon the face of the waters...it floated above the waters... Let there be firmament in the midst of the waters...Let the waters under the heaven be gathered together unto one place, and let the dry land appear...Let the waters bring forth abundantly the moving creature that hath life, and fowl that may fly above the Earth in the open firmament of heaven." Genesis 1:2ff.

According to this belief, water represented the nature of matter, just as the Spirit represented the nature of intelligence. The words, "If man is not reborn of the waters and of the Spirit" or "in water and in Spirit" might signify, "man is not born with his body and his soul." These words are echoed by Jesus words, "What is born of the flesh is flesh and what is born of Spirit is Spirit." Here Jesus established a clear distinction between body and Spirit. "What is born of the flesh" clearly indicates that only the body generates from the body and that the Spirit is independent.

The words from John Chapter 3 stand out. "The wind blows where it wishes and you hear the sound but know not from whence it comes nor whence it goes" are referring to the Spirit of God, who gives life, to whom He wishes, or rather to the soul of man. The words "you know not where it comes from nor where it goes," signifies that we do not know who the Spirit had been previously or who it will be in the future. If the Spirit or soul were created at the same time as the body, we would know where it came from because we would know its beginning. Whichever way you look at this passage, it confirms the principle of the pre-existence of the soul and subsequently the plurality of existences.

Even if the doctrine of reincarnation as expressed by John might be interpreted in principle in a purely mystic sense, the same could not happen with the passage in Matthew 11: 12-15, which does not permit any ambiguity, "He is Elias, who was to come." Here there is nothing figurative, nothing allegorical, only a complete affirmation.

Jesus explains them to us when He says, "If you wish to understand what I am saying, this is Elias who was to come." Therefore, if John was Elias, Jesus alluded to the time when John was living under the name of Elias.

"Till the present time the kingdom is seized by violence" is another allusion to the violence of the Mosaic laws, which ordered the extermination of infidels so that the rest might attain the Promised Land, the Paradise of the Hebrews, whereas according to the new law Heaven is won by charity and mildness.

Jesus then added in Matthew 11:15, "He that hath ears to hear, let him hear." These words are frequently uttered by Him, telling us that not everyone was in a condition to understand certain truths.

Jesus when speaking with his followers seems to provoke an answer that clearly speaks of reincarnation when and asks in Matthew 15:13, "who do people say the Son of man is?" They reply, "Some say Elijah who has come again or Jeremiah or one of the prophets." If that doesn't allude to reincarnation I don't know what does.

AND THOTH SAID

Great were my people in the ancient days,
great beyond the conception of the
little people now around me;

knowing the wisdom of old,
seeking far within the heart of infinity
knowledge that belonged to Earth's youth.
Wise were we with the wisdom
of the Children of Light who dwelt among us.
Strong were we with the power drawn
from the eternal fire.

In Matthew 3:11, John the Baptist says, "I baptize you with water, he shall baptize you with fire."

AND THOTH SAID

And of all these, greatest among the
children of men was my father, Thotme
keeper of the great temple,
link between the Children of Light,

Thotme is the Sumerian God Enki. Also, John 12:36 records the words of Jesus, "Believe in the light that you may be children of light."

AND THOTH SAID

[children of light] who dwelt within the temple and the
races of men who inhabited the ten islands.
Mouthpiece, after the Three,
of the Dweller of Unal,
speaking to the Kings
with the voice that must be obeyed.
Grew I there from a child into manhood,
being taught by my father the elder mysteries,
until in time there grew within the fire of wisdom,
until it burst into a consuming flame.

Thoth has a rich tradition to prepare his life as the ultimate servant of all of Atlantis. His father, Thotme, is identifiable with Enki, as well as The Dweller...who taught him the "elder mysteries." The he knowledge acquired at this level is wisdom so overwhelming that it is like an all-consuming fire. Much like many religions today speak of being "consumed by the fire of God" or the "unquenchable fire of the Holy Spirit."

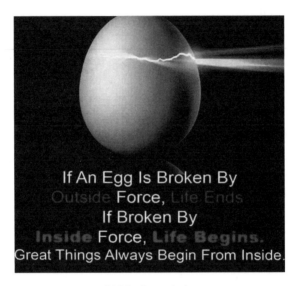

If An Egg Is Broken By
Outside Force, Life Ends
If Broken By
Inside Force, Life Begins.
Great Things Always Begin From Inside.

4biddenknowledge

AND THOTH SAID

Naught desired I but the attainment of wisdom.
Until on a great day the command came from the
Dweller of the Temple that I be brought before him.
Few there were among the children of men
who had looked upon that mighty face and lived,
for not as the sons of men are the
Children of Light when they are not incarnate
in a physical body.
Chosen was I from the sons of men,
taught by the Dweller so that his
purposes might be fulfilled.

Matthew 24:30 states, "And then shall appear the sign of the Son of man in heaven: and then shall all the tribes of the earth mourn, and they shall see the Son of man coming in the clouds of heaven with power and great glory." Thoth is about to come into his glory.

AND THOTH SAID

purposes yet unborn in the womb of time.
Long ages I dwelt in the Temple,
learning ever and yet ever more wisdom,
until I, too, approached the light emitted
from the great fire.

"Taught me he, the path to Amenti,
the underworld where the great king sits
upon his throne of might.
Deep I bowed in homage before the Lords of Life
and the Lords of Death,
receiving as my gift the Key of Life.
Free was I of the Halls of Amenti,
bound not by death to the circle of life.

In these words, Thoth explains that he has now overcome reincarnation. He has now achieved the ability to consciously incarnate at will or transfer his consciousness into a new body.

AND THOTH SAID

Far to the stars I journeyed until
space and time became as naught.
Then having drunk deep of the cup of wisdom,
I looked into the hearts of men and there found I
greater mysteries and was glad.
For only in the Search for Truth could my Soul
be stilled and the flame within be quenched.
Down through the ages I lived,
seeing those around me taste of the cup
of death and return again in the light of life.

Thoth has conquered the barriers of space and time or spacetime as we know it today. He is a space traveler, journeying "far to the stars." Through reincarnation or regeneration, he is ageless and immortal.

AND THOTH SAID

Gradually from the Kingdoms of Atlantis passed waves
of consciousness that had been one with me,
only to be replaced by spawn of a lower star.
In obedience to the law,
the word of the Master grew into flower.
Downward into the darkness turned the
thoughts of the Atlanteans,
Until at last in this wrath arose
from his Agwanti, the Dweller,

Agwanti has no English equivalent; it means a state of detachment.

AND THOTH SAID

speaking The Word, calling the power.
Deep in Earth's heart, the sons of Amenti heard,
and hearing, directing the changing of the flower of fire
that burns eternally, changing and shifting, using the Logos,
until that great fire changed its direction.
Over the world then broke the great waters,
drowning and sinking,
changing Earth's balance
until only the Temple of Light was left
standing on the great mountain on Undal
still rising out of the water;
some there were who were living,
saved from the rush of the fountains.
Called to me then the Master, saying:
Gather ye together my people.

By the power of the spoken word (the Logos), the world was altered and almost destroyed by fire and water. It is reminiscent of the Hebrew account of Noah and his Ark.   After the catastrophic global flood, Thoth gathers together his crew that he used in building the Egyptian civilization, after his father gave the order.

AND THOTH SAID

Take them by the arts ye have learned of far across the waters,
until ye reach the land of the hairy barbarians,
dwelling in caves of the desert.
Follow there the plan that ye know of.
Gathered I then my people and
entered the Great Ship of the Master.
Upward we rose into the morning.

The arts referred to are astronomy, architecture, sciences, alchemy, metaphysics, reading, and writing. The Great Ship is not an ocean-going vessel, it is a ship for the skies.

AND THOTH SAID

Dark beneath us lay the Temple.
Suddenly over it rose the waters.
Vanished from Earth,
until the time appointed,
was the great Temple.
Fast we fled toward the sun of the morning,
until beneath us lay the land of the children of Khem.

Image credit HiddenMeanings.com – Bill Donahue
On the left side of the image above you see a Vimana as depicted in
30,000-year-old Hindu texts.

AND THOTH SAID

Raging, they came with cudgels and spears,
lifted in anger seeking to slay
and utterly destroy the Sons of Atlantis.
Then raised I my staff and directed a ray of vibration,
striking them still in their tracks as fragments
of stone of the mountain.

Thoth provides us evidence of a weapon of unknown technology. Is it
a "ray-gun or some type of stun weapon or the use sonic or vibration
waves that was able to subdue the attackers? It is clearly unlike anything
known, even today.

The Active Denial System – Military.gov

The Active Denial System ads is needed in light of the fact that it's non-lethal and counter-work force system much more than the present day lethal weapons. The Active Denial System delivers the effects of a non-lethal weapon that has a similar impact on every single human target.

AND THOTH SAID

Then spoke I to them in words calm and peaceful,
telling them of the might of Atlantis,
saying we were children of the Sun and its messengers.

Thoth never said that they were gods. He always references himself as a son of man or a son of Atlantis.

AND THOTH SAID

Cowed I them by my display of magic-science
until at my feet they groveled, when I released them.
Long dwelt we in the land of KHEM,
long and yet long again.
Until obeying the commands of the Master,

who while sleeping yet lives eternally,"

Magic science translates into advanced technology that was most likely small devices that they were already carrying in their tool kit. For some 16,000 years, he ruled the ancient race of Egypt, from approximately 52,000 to 36,000 ago. At that time, the ancient barbarous race among which he and his followers had settled was elevated to a high degree of civilization. They slept in regeneration chambers for one hundred years at a time as they Astral-project and travel the universe.

AND THOTH SAID

I sent from me the Sons of Atlantis,
sent them in many directions,
that from the womb of time wisdom
might rise again in her children.
Long time dwelt I in the land of KHEM,
doing great works by the wisdom within me.

Thoth sent his crew to all continents to kick start new civilizations based on the same basic architecture and sciences. These Atlanteans were global and each ruler put a genetic marker on their humans, which created the different races we have today.

Another bible verse apparently copied from much older text seems to resonate with the words of Thoth is Ephesians 2:10, "For we are God's handiwork, created in Christ Jesus to do good works, which God prepared in advance for us to do."

AND THOTH SAID

Upward grew into the light of knowledge
the children of KHEM,
watered by the rains of my wisdom.
Blasted I then a path to Amenti so
that I might retain my powers,
living from age to age a Sun of Atlantis,
keeping the wisdom, preserving the records.
Great grew the sons of KHEM,
conquering the people around them,
growing slowly upwards in Soul force.

Now for a time I go from among them into
the dark halls of Amenti,
deep in the halls of the Earth,
before the Lords of the powers,
face to face once again with the Dweller.
Raised I high over the entrance, a doorway, a gateway
leading down to Amenti.
Few there would be with courage to dare it,
few pass the portal to dark Amenti.
Raised over the passage, I, a mighty pyramid,
using the power that overcomes Earth force.
Deep and yet deeper place I a force-house or chamber;
from it carved I a circular passage
reaching almost to the great summit.
There in the apex, set I the crystal,
sending the ray into the "Time-Space,"
drawing the force from out of the ether,
concentrating upon the gateway to Amenti.
Other chambers I built and left vacant to all seeming,
yet hidden within them are the keys to Amenti.

A 3D visualization of the Great Pyramid and its hidden chamber seen as white
dots. From Nature.com.

Cosmic-ray particles reveal secret chamber in Egypt's Great Pyramid as researchers have used muon detectors to discover a mysterious, thirty-meter long space. Physicists have used the by-products of cosmic rays to reveal a large, previously unidentified chamber inside the Great Pyramid in Giza, Egypt. Egyptologists have been quick to dismiss any idea of finding lost treasure in the lengthy void. "There's zero chance of hidden burial chambers," says Aidan Dodson, an Egyptologist at the University of Bristol, UK. The Great Pyramid was constructed by the pharaoh Khufu (also known as Cheops), who reigned from 2509–2483 BC. Constructed from limestone and granite blocks, and rising to 139 meters, it is the oldest and largest of the Giza pyramids and one of the most impressive structures to survive from the ancient world.

Whereas other pyramids from this period sit above underground burial chambers, Khufu's Pyramid contains several large rooms inside the body of the structure itself. These include the King's chamber, which still holds a stone sarcophagus, the smaller Queen's chamber and a sloping passageway known as the Grand Gallery.

These large chambers were discovered in the ninth century AD and explored extensively by Western archaeologists throughout the nineteenth century. Yet, enthusiasts have wondered ever since whether there might be more hidden chambers inside the pyramid, or even whether the king's real burial chamber is yet to be found. Material for this information is found at https//:www.Nature.com

AND THOTH SAID

He who in courage would dare the dark realms,
let him be purified first by long fasting.
Lie in the sarcophagus of stone in my chamber.
Then reveal I to him the great mysteries.
Soon shall he follow to where I shall meet him,
even in the darkness of Earth shall I meet him, I,
Thoth, Lord of Wisdom, meet him and hold him
and dwell with him always.

Jesus answered him, "Truly I tell you, today you will be with me in paradise." Luke 23:43

AND THOTH SAID

Builded I the Great Pyramid,

patterned after the pyramid of Earth force,
burning eternally so that it, too,
might remain through the ages.
In it, I builded my knowledge of Magic-Science.

The Great Pyramid is encoded with super advanced technology and
mathematics. Let's take a look at some of the wisdom that Thoth encoded
into the Great Pyramid. The Great Pyramid is a massive wireless power
plant. This is just one of many multifunctional purposes of this gigantic
stone computer here on Earth.

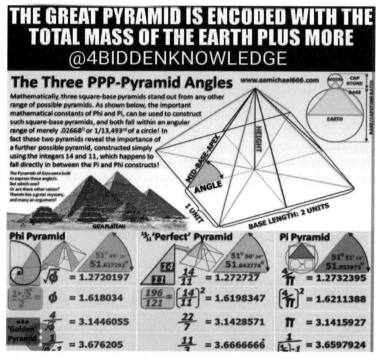

The curvature designed into the faces of the Great Pyramid exactly
matches the radius of the Earth. Equatorial Circumference of the Earth:
The Pyramid embodies a scale ratio of 1/43,200.

The perimeter of the base 43,200 = 24,734.94 miles, which is within 170
miles of the equatorial circumference of the earth.

Earth's Volume: The product of the pyramid's volume and density times
10^15 equal the ratio of volume to density of the earth. [10,339,823.3
cubic cubits * 0.4078994 * 10^15 = 4.21760772 x 10^21 cubic cubits =
259.93 x 10^9 cubic miles].

Earth's Mass: Mass of the pyramid = volume * density = 10,339,823.3 cubic cubits * 0.4078994 earth density = 4,217,497. The mass converted to pyramid tons = 4,217,607.72 * 1.25 = 5,272,010 pyramid tons.

Since the mean density of the earth was defined as 1.0, then the mass of the earth is 10^{15} times the mass in pyramid tons = 5.272 x 10^{21} pyramid tons = 5.99 x 10^{24} Kg.

Speed of Earth around the Sun: The Pyramid Inch times 10^8 = the speed of the earth around the sun, circa 2600 BCE.

Mass of the Earth: The weight of the pyramid is approximately 5,955,000 tons. Multiplied by 10^8 gives a reasonable estimate of the earth's mass.

Average Land Height: The average height of land above sea level for the earth is 5,449 inches. This is also the height of the pyramid.

The Light Equation: The height of the Great Pyramid, minus the height of the capstone represents one millionth the time it takes light to travel the mean radius of the earth's orbit around the sun (1 astronomical unit) using 1 Pyramid Inch equals 24 hours (mean solar day). [(5,813.2355653 - 103.0369176) /10^6 = .0057101986+ days = 493.36116 seconds = 8 minutes, 13.36 seconds]

The Velocity of Light: With distance of one A.U. known and the transit time of light for this same distance the velocity of light can be found. [91,848,816.9 miles / 493.36+ seconds = 186,169.5 miles/sec] The Velocity of Light: With distance of one A.U. known and the transit time of light for this same distance the velocity of light can be found. [91,848,816.9 miles / 493.36+ seconds = 186,169.5 miles/sec]

This is why they call me 4biddenknowledge!

This is me standing inside of the Grand Gallery of the Great Pyramid at Giza. The Grand Gallery inside of the Great Pyramid is located at 29.9972458 degrees North. The speed of light is exactly 299,972,458 meters per second. Coincidence??? I think not.

The Great Pyramid was a multi-functional, technological device. One of the many functions of a power plant. The Great Pyramid generated and transmitted wireless electricity. When I was inside the Great Pyramid in May 2014, I could feel the magnetic energy flowing through my body and I ascended up into the King's Chamber. The Great Pyramid was not built by Hebrew slaves as taught in school and church. Thoth built the Great Pyramid from the top down.

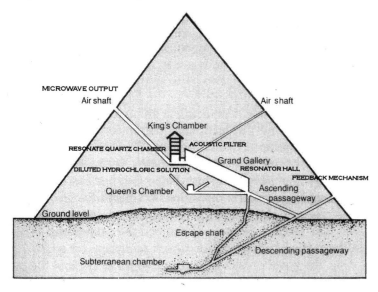

Image credit Christopher Dunn – The Giza Power Plant - Excellent Book.

AND THOTH SAID

So that I might be here when again I return from Amenti,
Aye, while I sleep in the Halls of Amenti,
my Soul roaming free will incarnate,
dwell among men in this form or another.
Emissary on Earth am I of the Dweller,
fulfilling his commands so many might be lifted.
Now return I to the halls of Amenti,
leaving behind me some of my wisdom.

Hermes, thrice-born is the strongest candidate for Thoth's mention of "my Soul roaming free will incarnate, dwell among men in this form or another." It is Hermes Trismegistus who is responsible for maintaining, secreting, and teaching of the single Emerald Tablet generally referred to until 1925.

AND THOTH SAID
Now, I depart from ye.
Know my commandments,
keep them and be them,
and I will be with you,
helping and guiding you into the Light.

Yet, another verse that made it into the bible from the Emerald Tablets. In John 14:15 Jesus says, "If you love me, keep my commandments." Also, Jesus speaks of how he will be a guiding Light to his disciples when he is gone, through the presence of the Great Comforter, known as the Holy Spirit.

AND THOTH SAID
Now before me opens the portal.
Go I down in the darkness of night.

Thoth enters the Halls of Amenti and will return in his physical form at a future time unknown to man. Does this sound familiar? The Bible says the same thing when Jesus promises to come again one day in the distant future to reclaim his rule over all his people.

CHAPTER FOUR

THE HALLS OF AMENTI

Emerald Tablet Two

AND THOTH SAID

Deep in Earth's heart lie the Halls of Amenti,
far 'neath the islands of sunken Atlantis,
Halls of the Dead and halls of the living,
bathed in the fire of the infinite All.

Far in a past time, lost in the space time,
the Children of Light looked down on the world.
Seeing the children of men in their bondage,
bound by the force that came from beyond.
Knew they that only by freedom from bondage
could man ever rise from the Earth to the Sun.

According to Thoth, only free-thinking individuals, using their own conscious thoughts, can be capable of rising up to a higher level of consciousness.

"Halls of Amenti" by Donny Arcade feature 4biddenknowledge – CrewZ – Richard Vagner. I own a record label and loved this tablet so much that my artists and I wrote a song about it. "Halls of Amenti" is available on all music apps.

AND THOTH SAID

Down they descended and created bodies,
taking the semblance of men as their own.
The Masters of everything said after their forming:
"We are they who were formed from the space-dust,
partaking of life from the infinite ALL;
living in the world as children of men,
like and yet unlike the children of men.

During later ages, the ego of Thoth passed into the bodies of men in the manner described in the tablets. As such, he incarnated three times, in his last being known as Hermes, the thrice-born.

Transfer Of Consciousness - Image Credit: 4biddenknowledge – Billy Carson

The 2045 Initiative is a nonprofit organization that develops a network and community of researchers in the field of life extension.

The main goal of the 2045 Initiative, as stated on its website, 2045.com, is "to create technologies enabling the transfer of an individual's personality to a more advanced non-biological carrier, and extending life, including to the point of immortality. We devote particular attention to enabling the fullest possible dialogue between the world's major spiritual traditions, science and society."

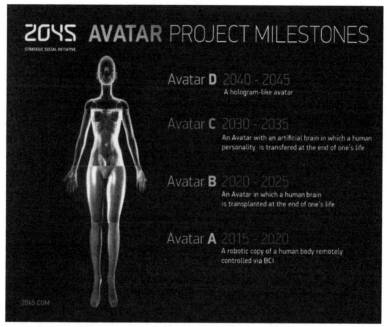

Avatar Project - Image Credit: 2045 Initiative

As evidenced by the information provided on 2045.com, it appears that we are following in the footsteps of the Atlanteans, who were seeking eternal life in the physical form. Take a look at some of the goals and initiatives being planned by the group at 2045.com:

From the year 2015 to 2020: 2045.com would like to create and supply the world with affordable android avatars that will be controlled by a system that links people's brains with computers.

2020-2025: They would like to create an autonomous life-support system in which a human brain can be taken out of a body and kept alive while being linked to a robotic avatar. Their hope is that a person whose body is failing them can live a full life.

2030-2035: The group at 2045.com wishes to create immortality by building a computer model of the brain that allows human consciousness to be transferred into the artificial carrier, giving everyone the possibility of cybernetic immortality.

2045: By this date, 2045.com would like to have established a new era for humanity in which the technological brains and transferred minds can receive new bodies with capabilities that far exceed the abilities of the human body.

According to the 2045 Initiative mission statement, the challenge for the immediate future is to prepare humanity for its greatest intellectual (attainment of higher consciousness) transition in history. "Today it is hard to imagine a future when bodies consisting of nanorobots will become affordable and capable of taking any form. It is also hard to imagine body holograms featuring controlled matter. One thing is clear however: humanity, for the first time in its history, will make a fully managed evolutionary transition and eventually become a new species. Moreover, prerequisites for a large-scale expansion into outer space will be created as well. An annual congress, "The Global Future, 2045" is organized by the 2045 Strategic Social Initiative to give a platform for discussing mankind's evolutionary strategy based on technologies of cybernetic immortality, as well as the possible impact of such technologies on global society, politics, and economies of the future." http://2045.com/about

Critics of Istkov and his associates, maintain that the brain is not reducible to bits of data transferable into a computer-like AI system and that such a reality is so far out of the reach of modern science as to make the project for immortality seem more like fantasy than reality. Or has it been done before the time of the scientific revolution and modernists are too afraid to acknowledge the possibilities such a project promises? https://www.telegraph.co.uk/tv/2016/03/16/why-no-amount-of-science-can-make-humans-immortal-horizon---revi/

Avatar and Machin

DARPA Reveals Avatar Program

The Defense Advanced Research Projects Agency (DARPA) is an agency of the United States Department of Defense responsible for the development of emerging technologies for use by the military. According to Sebastian Anthony of EXTREMETECH NEWS, the Avatar goal is to work on "interfaces and algorithms to enable a soldier to effectively partner with a semi-autonomous bipedal machine and allow it to act as the soldier's surrogate. DARPA wants to develop the walking equivalent of an unarmed aerial vehicle; a bipedal robot drone where the controlling soldier is hundreds or thousands of miles away from war front."

DARPA's goals for the Avatar program are not science fiction. The technology already exists to make it work. to pull it off. Check it out here:

https://www.extremetech.com/extreme/118773-darpa-reveals-avatar-program-robot-soldiers-incoming

AND THOTH SAID

Then for a dwelling place, far 'neath the earth crust,
blasted great spaces they by their power,
spaces apart from the children of men.
Surrounded them by forces and power,
shielded from harm they the Halls of the Dead.

This appears to refer to the history of the Thirty-two Masters and the plan they executed. They left their base reality and entered the holographic simulation we call our universe. They then proceed to transfer their consciousness into Avatars and build a great deep underground base of operations. The underground base was "blasted" out by superior earth boring technologies and then protected by a force field. Within this home base, they built the Halls of Amenti which appears to be powered by a crystal that directs energy emanating from the flower of life.

The crystal structure used is most likely an 8th dimensional Quasicrystal. By this method, they could project a 3 dimensional hologram of our entire universe.

The following link provides an indepth explanation of the graph-theoretic approach to quantum gravity and particle physics arriving at a quasicrystalline "possibility space." http://www.quantumgravityresearch.org/emergence-theory-overview

"The Great Pyramid of Giza can focus electromagnetic energy in its hidden rooms. Boffins from ITMO University and the Laser Zentrum Hannover found that the 481-foot building is capable of creating pockets of higher energy in its inner rooms and at its base. The research group plans to use the results to design nanoparticles, which will be used to develop sensors and highly efficient solar cells," reports, *The Journal of Applied Physics* 124, 034903 (2018). Dr. Andrey Evlyukhin, scientific supervisor and coordinator of the study said, "We decided to look at the Great Pyramid as a particle dissipating radio waves resonantly. There is also a third, unfinished chamber beneath the base of the huge structure. The team's analysis shows that the powerful pyramid concentrates electromagnetic energy in its internal chambers." Complete your research of this subject at:

https://www.eurekalert.org/pub_releases/2018-07/iu-srt073018.php

and

https://aip.scitation.org/doi/10.1063/1.5026556

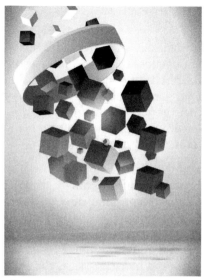

Emergence Theory Concept Picture

Emergence Theory

Emergence Theory is a quantum-gravity-unification theory that brings together quantum mechanics, general, and special relativity. At the root of emergence theory is the idea that the whole of reality is made of information that must follow rules and be enacted upon by a "user." According to the theory, information is defined as symbols that convey meaning. Codes and languages are examples of symbols that convey meaning. These symbols and meanings must then follow rules. For example, words must be arranged in certain ways to create communication. Lastly, a "chooser" or some form of consciousness must exist to interact with the information and choose how it is used.

Speaking of language and codes, science has observed that realty is geometric at all scales. Additionally, some scientists hypothesize that all meaning in our physical reality is expressed through an entirely geometric language or code using symbolism. Bring the mathematics of quasicrystals into it and a more complete picture can be seen. For instance, think of how movies are composed of single frames. Each frame is complete and has the potential to be full of meaning. Combine several movie frames at a particular speed and the frames disappear into a fluidity of patterns that appear seamless. Over many of these frames, patterns emerge on the 3D quasicrystal. These patterns become more and more meaningful and sophisticated with time. Gradually patterns resembling and acting as particles form on the quasicrystal. With time, these particles take on more and more complex forms, and eventually the reality we all know and love emerges, just as the story of a movie unfolds.

Besides codes and languages, space-time also comes into play when speaking of the Emergence theory. Building on Einstein's space-time model, in which the future and past exist simultaneously in one geometric object, Emergence theory views spacetime in similar ways. This theory states that there is a dynamic, constant, and causality loop relationship between all moments in time, in which the past influences the future and the future influences the past.

Einstein's space-time theories come to the fore in realizing emergence theory as viewing past and future events existing at the same time in a single geometric reality. Our consciousness emerges in such a construct and exists in all three dimensional quasicrystals comparable to tiny observers allowing for the development of higher levels of thought. These continue to expand and grow and spread out like the petals of a flower, becoming larger and more possessive of the space around them until they occupy the furthest areas of the universe. In such a scenario, it would not be far fetched to realize mankind occupying vast spaces within an innumerable cadre of galaxies, becoming as it were, a giant neural network. The collective consciousness takes on new meaning in this model.

The complete and more thorough examination of emergence theory and consciousness can be found at the following link: http://www. quantumgravityresearch.org/emergence-theory-overview

AND THOTH SAID
Side by side then, placed they other spaces,
filled them with Life and with Light from above.
Builded they then the Halls of Amenti,
that they might dwell eternally there,
living with life to eternity's end.

Thirty and two were there of the children,
sons of Lights who had come among men,
seeking to free from the bondage of darkness
those who were bound by the force from beyond.

Deep in the Halls of Life grew a flower, flaming,
expanding, driving backward the night.

Placed in the centre, a ray of great potence, Life
giving, Light giving, filling with power all who came near it.
Placed they around it thrones, two and thirty,
places for each of the Children of Light,
placed so that they were bathed in the radiance,
filled with the Life from the eternal Light.

Open your EYE. These are flower of life representations which are
encoded with the 64-grid tetrahedrons parallax. However, these are
actually 2-dimensional representations of a 3-dimensional structure.
This structure is actually a shadow being laid down by an 8th dimensional
quasicrystal. This shadow is what we call "the entire universe," creating
a matrix in which we are all fully immersed. Ancient civilizations left us
a pattern to follow all over the entire planet.

Courtesy of 4biddenknowledge

AND THOTH SAID

There time after time placed they their first created bodies
so that they might be filled with the Spirit of Life.
One hundred years out of each thousand must the
Life-giving Light flame forth on their bodies.
Quickening, awakening the Spirit of Life.

There in the circle from aeon to aeon,
sit the Great Masters,
living a life not known among men.
There in the Halls of Life they lie sleeping;
free flows their Soul through the bodies of men.

Time after time, while their bodies lie sleeping,
incarnate they in the bodies of men.
Teaching and guiding onward and upward,
out of the darkness into the light.

You can see here in these passages that the Atlantean lords have the ability to occupy biological avatars while their bodies are in a state of deep meditation in the Halls of Amenti. Regeneration (quickening, awakening) could also be a prerequisite to entering a higher form of consciousness that enables the believer to fall into a deep meditation. The passage concludes that regardless of the state of meditation, the believer will always be moving onward and upward toward the light.

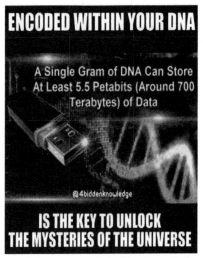

Image Courtesy Of 4biddenknowledge

Many believe that the Anunnaki and Atlanteans genetically modified proto-modern humans on this planet to become *Homo sapiens sapiens*. Prior to the proliferation of our species, the earth was being more and more populated by two other species of "wise" people, *Homo sapiens idaltu* and *Homo sapiens neanderthalensis*. Oddly enough, it is generally accepted by most scientists today that *Homo sapiens sapiens* were the primary occupants of planet earth about 50,000 years ago, a number that fits dramatically in the Thoth narrative. This genetic modification significantly increased the modern human DNA capacity for the gathering and maintaining information. What modern scientists are calling worthless DNA is anything but. There is a message written on that DNA and it was purposely disconnected by the Anunnaki to prevent humans from reaching Supreme Higher Realms of Consciousness and Superior Intelligence. You are a breathing, walking hard drive with trillions of terabytes of data on your biological hard drive. At Harvard's Wyss Institute, two geneticists and bioengineers, have basically relegated DNA as comparative to a digital storage device. One gram of DNA can store 7000 gigabytes of data. The work, carried out by George Church and Sri Kosuri, treats DNA as just another digital storage device. That means there is enough room for information storage in a smidgen of DNA that would fit on the tip of a frog's tail. Check up on the fascinating aspects of these Harvard scientists at this link: http://www.extremetech.com/extreme/134672-harvard-cracks-dna-storage-crams-700-terabytes-of-data-into-a-single-gram

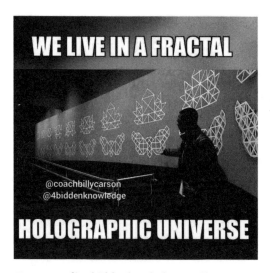

Image credit 4biddenkowledge – Billy Carson

"We are living in a fractal, holographic matrix. A fully immersed hologram in a Holographic Universe. The edges of our universe are two dimensional planes that form a three dimensional form that is projecting the holographic fractals of which we are a part of, and in which your spirit is currently trapped. Your spirit is outside this spacetime model and is being broadcast like a radio frequency. None of us are actually here. This is a Third Dimension matrix, producing a type of temporal consciousness." https://www.arjonline.org/papers/arjb/v3-i1/4.pdf

In the book, *The Holographic Universe,* by Michael Talbot, the author teaches that we are living in a holographic matrix. "Thought or internal consciousness materializes reality on this planet as a vibrating light (hologram) is brought in through an electromagnetic frequency (vibration/sound). Thus, what we see or think of as a solid reality is a hologram created through thought, light, and sound. Everything in this material world is here because our Higher Light Frequency of Self has called everything into being. We are a Collective Consciousness of Everything Created. Our particles instantaneously communicate with one another regardless of distance. Whether we are ten feet or ten billion miles apart, somehow each particle always seems to know what the other is doing. All information is possessed by the Whole and although we think we are separate from this whole, we are not. Separation is an illusion. The whole of all that exist cannot be separated. We are a part of a fractal of light that makes up this entire Third Dimension and this Holographic Universe, which was designed by our ancestor civilization. These ancestors are most likely the Atlanteans of old. We are the SIMS. Your consciousness wave function collapses electromagnetic energy into quantified digital bits of information we call matter." www.ontheroadtofindout.ca/fractals-holographics.htm

According to Robert Skopec, "We are probably living in a fractal holographic matrix. The edges of our Universe are two-dimensional planes that form a three-dimensional dodecahedron that is projecting the holographic fractals of which we are a part of and in which your spirit is currently trapped in. The spirit is outside of this space-time model and is being broadcast in like a radio frequency. None of us are actually here. This third dimensional matrix appears to be a type of Temporal Consciousness Prison. Thus, what we see or think of as a solid reality is a hologram created through thought, light, and sound. Everything in this material world is here because our Higher Light Frequency of Self has called them into being. Like in a video game the next frame of graphics appears as the characters on the screen need them to. We are a Collective Consciousness of Everything Created. Our particles instantaneously communicate with one another regardless of distance. Thanks to Quantum Entanglement Entropy each particle seems to know what the others is doing. All information is possessed by the Whole despite we think we are separate from this Whole, in reality we are not. Separation is an illusion, and thanks to Quantum Entanglement Entropy, we cannot be separated from the Whole. We are a part of a fractal of light that makes up this entire third dimension and this Holographic Universe." *NeuroQuantology* | June 2017 | Volume 15 | Issue 2 | Page

200-207 | doi: 10.14704/nq.2017.15.2.1030   Skopec R., "Coding by Quantum Entanglement Entropy."

Can the existence of our consciousness be the gift from our Atlantean space travelers?

AND THOTH SAID

There in the Hall of Life, filled with their wisdom,
known not to the races of man, living forever 'neath the cold
fire of life, sit the Children of Light.
Times there are when they awaken,
come from the depths to be lights among men,
infinite they among finite men.

The Atlantean lords had the ability to astral project from their regenerating avatars and enter the Matrix, so to speak. They had the ability to engage humankind, even from the astral form. They would keep their avatars young by maintaining a strict regimen of physical time inside the Halls of Amenti regeneration chambers. Remember, Thoth claims to have descended 10 times into the chamber, while spending 100 years inside the chamber each time. That means he has spent a total of 10,000 years in regeneration of his physical avatars. These lords also have unlimited access to the Halls of Amenti for use at any time that they see fit.

AND THOTH SAID

He who by progress has grown from the darkness,
lifted himself from the night into light,
free is he made of the Halls of Amenti,
free of the Flower of Light and of Life.
Guided he then, by wisdom and knowledge,
passes from men, to the Master of Life.

There he may dwell as one with the Masters,
free from the bonds of the darkness of night.
Seated within the flower of radiance sit seven
Lords from the Space-Times above us,
helping and guiding through infinite Wisdom,

the pathway through time of the children of men.

Image Courtesy of 4biddenknowledge

Mighty and strange, they,
veiled with their power,
silent, all-knowing,
drawing the Life force,
different yet one with the

children of men.
Aye, different, and yet One
with the Children of Light.
Custodians and watchers of the force of man's bondage,
ready to loose when the light has been reached.

They are waiting for us to grow up. Mankind is still and infant. We have not even begun to crawl yet. A very good sign that we are ready will be when the 7.5 billion rise up together and remove the 100 elite families that are running the planet.

AND THOTH SAID
First and most mighty,
sits the Veiled Presence, Lord of Lords,
the infinite Nine,
over the other from each
the Lords of the Cycles;

Three, Four, Five, and Six, Seven, Eight,
each with his mission, each with his powers,
guiding, directing the destiny of man.
There sit they, mighty and potent,
free of all time and space.

Thoth went to the land of Khem which later chose its capitol to be
Hermopolis, also known as Khemenu. The Egyptian name of the city,
means "eight-town," after the Ogdoad, a group of eight "primordial"
deities whose prehistoric cult had once dominated there.

AND THOTH SAID
Not of this world they,
yet akin to it,
Elder Brothers they,
of the children of men.
Judging and weighing,
they with their wisdom,
watching the progress
of Light among men.

As you can see from the several verses above. The Atlantean lords are secretly guiding and managing mankind from the underground base. They claim to be helping raise man back to a high level of civilization and high level of consciousness. These are the watchers of old.

Image credit 4biddenknowledge

Did you know that the Great Pyramid has eight sides? This is not a well-known fact. The central lines of each side from base to peak have a concave nature, creating eight sides instead of four.

AND THOTH SAID

There before them was I led by the Dweller,
watched him blend with One from above.
Then from HE came forth a voice saying:
'Great art thou, Thoth, among children of men.
Free henceforth of the Halls of Amenti,

Master of Life among children of men.
Taste not of death except as thou will it,
drink thou of Life to Eternity's end,
Henceforth forever is Life,
thine for the taking.
Henceforth is Death at the call of thy hand.

The Atlanteans have been given eternal life. Not by magic or by the power of God. But by wisdom and understanding on how to manipulate energy and the ether itself.

AND THOTH SAID

Dwell here or leave here when thou desireth,
free is Amenti to the 'Sun of man.'

Notice the spelling of "SUN". This is a reference to the Sun from the
Atlantean home world. They are the only ones with access to the Halls
of Amenti.

AND THOTH SAID

Then from his throne came one of the Masters,
taking my hand and leading me onward,
through all the Halls of the deep hidden land.
Led he me through the Halls of Amenti,
showing the mysteries that are known not to man.

Through the dark passage, downward he led me,
into the Hall where site the dark Death.
Vast as space lay the great Hall before me,
walled by darkness but yet filled with Light.

Before me arose a great throne of darkness,
veiled on it seated a figure of night.
Darker than darkness sat the great figure,
dark with a darkness not of the night.
Before it then paused the Master, speaking

The Word that brings about Life, saying;
'Oh, master of darkness,
guide of the way from Life unto Life,
before thee I bring a Sun of the morning.
Touch him not ever with the power of night.
Call not his flame to the darkness of night.
Know him, and see him,
one of our brothers,
lifted from darkness into the Light.
Release thou his flame from its bondage,

free let it flame through the darkness of night.'
Raised then the hand of the figure,
forth came a flame that grew clear and bright.
Rolled back swiftly the curtain of darkness,
unveiled the Hall from the darkness of night.

Then grew in the great space before me,
flame after flame, from the veil of the night.
Uncounted millions leaped they before me,
' some flaming forth as flowers of fire.

Some there were that faded swiftly;
others that grew from a small spark of light.
Each surrounded by its dim veil of darkness,
yet flaming with light that could never be quenched.
Coming and going like fireflies in springtime,
filled they with space with Light and with Life.

Then spoke a voice, mighty and solemn, saying:
'These are lights that are souls among men,
growing and fading, existing forever,
changing yet living, through death into life.
When they have bloomed into flower,
reached the zenith of growth in their life,
swiftly then send I my veil of darkness,
shrouding and changing to new forms of life.'
So grows the soul of man ever upward,
quenched yet unquenched by the darkness of night.
I, Death, come, and yet I remain not,
for life eternal exists in the All;
only an obstacle, I in the pathway,
quick to be conquered by the infinite light.
Awaken, O flame that burns ever inward,
flame forth and conquer the veil of the night.

Then in the midst of the flames

in the darkness grew there one that
drove forth the night, flaming, expanding,
ever brighter, until at last was nothing but Light.

Then spoke I:
O, great master,
let me be a teacher of men,
leading then onward and upward until they,
too, are lights among men;
freed from the veil of the night that surrounds them,
flaming with light that shall shine among men.

Spoke to me then the voice:
Go, as yet will. So be it decreed.
Master are ye of your destiny,
free to take or reject at will.
Take yet the power, take ye the wisdom.
Shine as a light among the children of men.

THE KEY OF WISDOM

Emerald Tablet Three

AND THOTH SAID
I, Thoth, the Atlantean,
give of my wisdom,
give of my knowledge,
give of my power.
Give that they, too, might have wisdom
to shine through the world...

Wisdom is power, and power is wisdom,
one with each other, perfecting the whole.

Be thou not proud, O man, in thy wisdom.
Discourse with the ignorant, as well as the wise.
If one comes to thee full of knowledge,
listen and heed, for wisdom is all."

In the article, "Thought, Pride and Arrogance," Gyan Rajhans eloquently defines these ideas in step with Thoth's admonitions. "Pride rears its head even in the most unsuspected corners. One man may be proud that he is proud, and another, proud that he is not proud. While one may be proud that he is a non-believer in God, another may be proud of his devotion to God. Learning may render one man proud, and yet ignorance can also be the source of pride for another man. Ego is nothing but pride in its inflated form." Rajhans Quote from: https://www.thoughtco.com/pride-ego-and-arrogance-1770589

AND THOTH SAID
Keep thou not silent when evil is spoken for Truth
like the sunlight shines above all.

He who over-steppeth the Law shall be punished,
for only through Law comes the freedom of men.
Cause thou not fear for fear is a bondage,
a fetter that binds the darkness to men.

Thoth is empowering humans to speak up when injustice, wrong doings, racism, unfair treatment and any other evil thing that is happening around us. The law is the law of Karmic energy.

AND THOTH SAID

Follow thine heart during thy lifetime.
Do thou more than is commanded of thee.
When thou hast gained riches,
follow thou thine heart,
for all these are of no avail if
thine heart be weary.
Diminish thou not the time of
following thine heart.
It is abhorred of the soul.

They that are guided go not astray,
but they that are lost cannot find a straight path.
If thou go among men, make for thyself,
Love, the beginning and end of the heart.

If one cometh unto thee for council,
let him speak freely,
that the thing for which he hath
come to thee may be done.
If he hesitates to open his heart to thee,
it is because thou, the judge, doeth the wrong.
Repeat thou not extravagant speech,
neither listen thou to it,
for it is the utterance of one
not in equilibrium.
Speak thou not of it,

so that he before thee may know wisdom.

Silence is of great profit.
An abundance of speech profiteth nothing.
Exalt not thine heart above the children of men,
lest it be brought lower than the dust.

Another verse from the Bible that some believe originate in the Emerald Tablets, "It is the spirit that quickeneth; the flesh profiteth nothing: the words that I speak unto you, they are spirit, and they are life." John 6:63. How familiar do the words of Thoth sound when he says if one finds riches, but cannot lose his weariness? As found in the Bible, "What does it profit a man, if he loses his soul." When someone comes for your counsel and cannot be satisfied, it is you who have done wrong. Also, don't speak aloud with extravagant speech. No one appreciates the boisterous talk of the ignorant. Above, simply to talk, talk, talk is of no value when silence can bring true riches. It is easy to see the fairness in the words of Thoth.

AND THOTH SAID

If thou be great among men,
be honoured for knowledge and gentleness.
If thou seeketh to know the nature of a friend,
ask not his companion,
but pass a time alone with him. Debate with him,
testing his heart by his words and his bearing.

That which goeth into the storehouse must come forth,
and the things that are thine must be shared with a friend.

Knowledge is regarded by the fool as ignorance,
and the things that are profitable are to him hurtful.
He liveth in death.
It is therefore his food.

As we can see here, greatness is about possessing knowledge and wisdom. This idea is parallel to the teachings of the Apostle Paul in biblical times. In I Corinthians 1:18 he writes, "Hath not God made foolish the wisdom of this world?" In other words, true Knowledge cannot be perceived by the average person who perceives it to be foolishness...Christians teach the Knowledge of the Light found in Jesus, which to the rest of the world is foolishness.

The Key of Wisdom by 4biddenknowledge – Now Available On All Music Stores

AND THOTH SAID

The wise man lets his heart overflow
but keeps silent his mouth.
O man, list to the voice of wisdom;
list to the voice of light.

Mysteries there are in the Cosmos
that unveiled fill the world with their light.
Let he who would be free from the bonds of darkness
first divine the material from the immaterial,
the fire from the earth;
for know ye that as earth descends to earth,

so also fire ascends unto
fire and becomes one with fire.
He who knows the fire that is within
himself shall ascend unto the eternal fire

and dwell in it eternally.

Fire, the inner fire,
is the most potent of all force,
for it overcometh all things and
penetrates to all things of the Earth.
Man supports himself only on that which resists.
So Earth must resist man else he existeth not.

All eyes do not see with the same vision,
for to one an object appears of
one form and color
and to a different eye of another.
So also the infinite fire,
changing from color to color,
is never the same from day to day.

Thus, speak I, THOTH, of my wisdom,
for a man is a fire burning bright
through the night;
never is quenched in the veil of the darkness,
never is quenched by the veil of the night.
Into men's hearts, I looked by my wisdom,
found them not free from the bondage of strife.
Free from the toils, thy fire, O my brother,
lest it be buried in the shadow of night!

Hark ye, O man, and list to this wisdom:
where do name and form cease?
Only in consciousness, invisible,
an infinite force of radiance bright
The forms that ye create by brightening

they vision are truly effects that follow thy cause.

Man is a star bound to a body,
until in the end, he is freed through his strife.
Only by struggle and toiling thy
utmost shall the star within thee
bloom out in new life.
He who knows the commencement of all things,

ree is his star from the realm of night.

We are all beings of photonic light, temporarily trapped in a physical body. We are here to learn and seek wisdom. Those that do not acquire wisdom and understanding are set to reincarnate back into the cycle over and again. Those that learn life's lessons and gain knowledge and wisdom will be set free from the reincarnation cycle and may be able to consciously incarnate at will anywhere in the universe.

AND THOTH SAID
Remember, O man, that all which exists
is only another form of that which exists not.
Everything that has being is passing into yet other
being and thou thyself are not an exception.

In this passage, Thoth is referencing what we know as physics. The Second Law of Thermodynamics states that the state of entropy of the entire universe, as an isolated system, will always increase over time. The second law also states that the changes in the entropy in the universe can never be negative. Energy cannot be destroyed. It can only be transformed. https://chem.libretexts.org/

AND THOTH SAID
Consider the Law, for all is Law.
Seek not that which is not of the Law,
for such exists only in the illusions of the senses.
Wisdom cometh to all her children
even as they cometh unto wisdom.

All through the ages,
the light has been hidden.
Awake, O man, and be wise.

Deep in the mysteries of life have I traveled,
seeking and searching for that which is hidden.
List ye, O man, and be wise.
Far 'neath the earth crust,
in the Halls of Amenti,
mysteries I saw that are hidden from men.

Oft have I journeyed the deep hidden passage,
looked on the Light that is Life among men.
There 'neath the flowers of Life ever living,
searched I the hearts and the secrets of men.
Found I that man is but living in darkness,
light of the great fire is hidden within.

Masters are they of the great Secret Wisdom,
brought from the future of infinity's end.
Seven are they, the Lords of Amenti,
overlords they of the Children of Morning,
Suns of the Cycles, Masters of Wisdom...

Formed are not they as the children of men?
Three, Four, Five and Six, Seven, Eight,
Nine are the titles of the Masters of men.

Far from the future, formless yet forming,
came they as teachers for the children of men.
Live they forever, yet not of the living,
bound not to life and yet free from death.

Rule they forever with infinite wisdom,
bound yet not bound to the dark Halls of Death.
Life they have in them, yet life that is not life,

free from all are the Lords of the ALL.

Forth from them came forth the Logos,
instruments they of the power o'er all.
Vast is their countenance,
yet hidden in smallness,
formed by a forming, known yet unknown.

Three holds the key of all hidden magic,
creator he of the halls of the Dead...
sending forth power, shrouding with darkness,
binding the souls of the children of men;
sending the darkness, binding the soul force;
director of negative to the children of men.

Four is he who looses the power...
Lord, he, of Life to the children of men.
Light is his body, flame is his countenance;
freer of souls to the children of men.

Five is the master, the Lord of all magic
Key to The Word that resounds among men...

Six is the Lord of Light, the hidden pathway,
path of the souls of the children of men...

Seven is he who is Lord of the vastness,
master of Space and the key of the Times...

Eight is he who orders the progress;
weighs and balances the journey of men

NINE is the father, vast he of countenance,
forming and changing from out of the formless.

The Egyptian Museum in Cairo. The country's ancient relics were once a cornerstone of a thriving tourism sector. Photograph: Khaled Elfiqi/EPA

In the Cairo Museum is displayed one of Egypt's most enigmatic coffins. It is called the Coffin of Petamon. The inscriptions found chiseled fuel the imagination of anyone who investigates. They read: "I am One that transforms into Two, I am Two that transforms into Four, I am Four that transforms into Eight, After this I am One."

The Octave of Creation

The Octagenic Stone of the alchemists, only recently glimpsed by modern people, is part of the fundamental matrix of reality described in the Emerald Tablets and represents an archetypal template from which diverse modern mystical and religious symbols have emerged. How did the ancients view the Stone? The Egyptian Octad, or eight qualities of creation, was worshipped in the temples of Hermopolis, where Thoth was regarded as the head of the Group of Eight and was responsible for enabling them to come into existence. Thoth inventor of the musical octave is responsible for embedding it in the mathematics of the universe. The sacred name of Hermopolis, Khemenu, means the City of Eight, and is possibly the origin of our word alchemy. According to the ancient Egyptian papyri, the ultimate act of creation was the Eighth, which returned directly to the One: I am the One that transforms into Two; I am the Two that transforms into Four; I am the Four that transforms into Eight; After this am I One again. We now recognize this ancient sequence as the dance of life itself. In the division of every human cell, a process known as mitosis takes place that involves a sequence of the Seven Steps of Transformation resulting in an equal dividing of genetic material, and in the Eight Step, the creation of a new cell also known in modern science as 'Mitosis.' This research from: The Emerald Tablet: Alchemy of Personal Transformation, by Dennis Hauck.

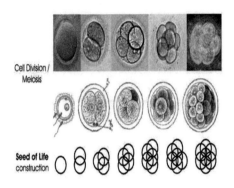

Image Credit - World Mysteries – Blog

"The symbol for the Seed of Life is a ubiquitous sacred geometric symbol. The Seed of Life was even deemed the "Egg of Life" and "Fruit of Life," a direct reference once again to our primordial egg. The Seed of Life is said to be a reflection or geometric expression of the story of creation with God doing his mighty work in six days and resting on the seventh or Sabbath, the same motif we used to discover the cryptogram or cipher for the English Alphabet. The Seed of Life is created by adding one circle a day to the original egg or sphere of creation, with the second day, creating our ever-present Vesica Piscis, what we deemed as the Vessel of the Pi Scission. Symbolically, this entire process reflects the process of cell division that we see in human reproduction called Meiosis."

http://blog.world-mysteries.com/ancient-writings/cracking-pi-part-3/

AND THOTH SAID
Meditate on the symbols I give thee.
Keys are they, though hidden from men.

Reach ever upward, O Soul of the morning.
Turn thy thoughts upward to Light and to Life.
Find in the keys of the numbers I bring thee,
light on the pathway from life unto life.

Seek ye with wisdom.
Turn thy thoughts inward.
Close not thy mind to the flower of Light.
Place in thy body a thought-formed picture.
Think of the numbers that lead thee to Life.

Clear is the pathway to he who has wisdom.
Open the door to the Kingdom of Light.

Pour forth thy flame as a Sun of the morning.
Shut out the darkness and live in the day.

Take thee, O man! As part of thy being,
the Seven who are but are not as they seem.
Opened, O man! Have I my wisdom.
Follow the path in the way I have led.

Masters of Wisdom,
SUN of the MORNING LIGHT and LIFE
to the children of men.

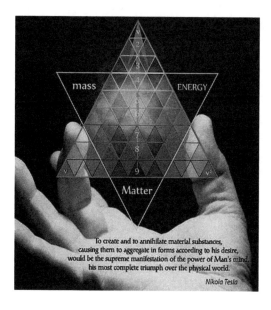

To create and to annihilate material substances,
causing them to aggregate in forms according to his desire,
would be the supreme manifestation of the power of Man's mind,
his most complete triumph over the physical world.

Nikola Tesla

I'm sure you have all heard this famous quote from Nikola Tesla, "If you only knew the magnificence of the 3, 6, and 9, then you would have a key to the universe." But did you know that the equinox and solstices are in March June and September? These months are 3 6 and 9! Could this be the key Tesla was referring to? There must be some great power to these events since almost every ancient civilization had structures made for these occurrences.

Image credit Sacred Teachings

CHAPTER SIX

THE SPACE BORN

Emerald Tablet Four

Astral Travel and The Merkabah

AND THOTH SAID

List ye, O man, to the voice of wisdom,
list to the voice of THOTH, the Atlantean.
Freely I give to thee of my wisdom,
gathered from the time and space of this cycle;
master of mysteries, SUN of the morning,
living forever, a child of the LIGHT,
shining with brightness, star of the morning.

Thoth is referring to the cyclical rise and fall of civilizations. Just as the Mayans believed that there have already been four worlds, and that we are moving into the fifth world now as we enter the age of Aquarius.

AND THOTH SAID

THOTH the teacher of men, is of ALL.
Long time ago, I in my childhood,
lay 'neath the stars on long-buried ATLANTIS,
dreaming of mysteries far above men.

Then in my heart grew there a great longing to
conquer the pathway that led to the stars.
Year after year, I sought after wisdom,
seeking new knowledge, following the way,
until at last my SOUL, in great travail,

broke from its bondage and bounded away.

The above statement refers to astral projection, also known as an out-of-body experience.

Image courtesy of Pantheon Elite Records – Song entitled "The Astral" by CrewZ with Donny Arcade.

The configuration of the Star Tetrahedron is formed within the first eight cells of life and remains fixed at the base of the spine throughout one's life. Known in esoteric knowledge of ancient Egypt as the Merkaba (Mer = Light, Ka = Spirit, Ba = Body). The star tetrahedron also models the energetic body of the human being, the blending of heaven and earth, male and female. The tetrahedron is ubiquitous throughout nature because the 64 tetrahedron grid is the structure of the vacuum (the fabric of space). This is also the basis for the Jewish Star Of David. It actually has nothing to do with stars in the sky. It's the inner star. This symbol can also be found on glyphs in Egypt. Thoth is depicted with this symbol in his left hand in the Emerald Tablets Of Thoth.

See a picture of the Merkabah on my Instagram post:

http://4biddnknowledge.tumblr.com/post/96052081456/
the-configuration-of-the-startetrahedron-is

Thoth appears to have mastered the use of the Merkabah. Historically, the Merkabah has been viewed as a "chariot "or vehicle that allows a person to ascend into higher worlds or descend into lower worlds. In actuality, however, the Mer-Ka-Bah is much more than a vehicle that escorts people to different worlds; it's a primal pattern attributed with creating all things and all universes, visible and invisible. For more information, read The Ancient Secret of the Flower of Life, Volumes I & II by Drunvalo Melchizedek.

"In the Bible, there is reference to Ezekiel and the wheels by which Ezekiel ascended into heaven. This was the Mer-ka-Ba. In the Torah, there is reference to the Merkavah (as it is spelled in Hebrew), which has two different meanings: One meaning is "chariot," which is a vehicle; the other is the "Throne of God." When the two definitions are combined, the true meaning comes to life. In Ancient Egypt, this primal pattern was called the MerKaBa. It was actually three words, not one. Mer meant a kind of light that rotated within itself. Ka meant spirit, in this case referring to the human spirit. Ba meant the human body, though it also could mean the concept of Reality that spirit holds. And so, the entire word in ancient Egypt referred to a rotating light that would take the spirit and the body from one world into   another."   https://infiniteshift.wordpress.com/2015/04/03/
the-meaning-of-the-merkaba-drunvalo-melchizedek/

Thoth and Civilizations

AND THOTH SAID
Free was I from the bondage of earth-men.
Free from the body, I flashed through the night.
Unlocked at last for me was the star-space.
Free was I from the bondage of night.

Now to the end of space sought I wisdom,
far beyond knowledge of finite man.

Far into space, my SOUL traveled freely

into infinity's circle of light.
Strange, beyond knowledge, were some of the planets,
great and gigantic, beyond dreams of men.

Yet found I Law, in all of its beauty, working
through and among them as here among men.

Flashed forth my soul through infinity's beauty,
far through space
I flew with my thoughts.

Rested I there on a planet of beauty.
Strains of harmony filled all the air.

Shapes there were, moving in Order,
great and majestic as stars in the night;
mounting in harmony, ordered equilibrium,
symbols of the Cosmic, like unto Law.

Many the stars I passed in my journey,
many the races of men on their worlds;
some reaching high as stars of the morning,
some falling low in the blackness of night.

Each and all of them struggling upward,
gaining the heights and plumbing the depths,
moving at times in realms of brightness,
living through darkness, gaining the Light.

Know, O man, that Light is thine heritage.
Know that darkness is only a veil.
Sealed in thine heart is brightness eternal,
waiting the moment of freedom to conquer,
waiting to rend the veil of the night.

Some I found who had conquered the ether.

Free of space were they while yet they were men.

Using the force that is the foundation of ALL things,
far in space constructed they a planet,
drawn by the force that flows through the ALL;
condensing, coalescing the ether into forms,
that grew as they willed.

Thoth had come across men in civilizations so advanced that they had mastered control over the fabric of spacetime. He traversing the universe in speeds unimaginable, encountering falling and ascending civilizations. He finds beauty and harmony in faraway worlds. This is a direct reference to a type 2 civilization, which is able to build a Dyson Sphere. www.ascensionwithearth.com/2017_03_16_archive.html

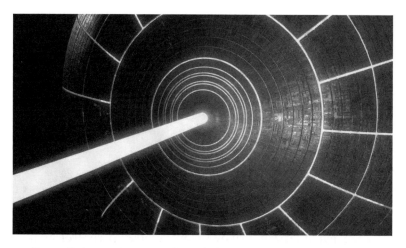

Dyson Sphere - Image credit – 4biddenknowledge – Billy Carson

Types of Civilizations

According to Russian astrophysicist, Nikolai Kardashev, civilizations can be separated into classifications according their energetic consumption and disposal. For example, humans eat dead plants and meats which sustains our energetic needs. Therefore, according to Kardashev, we are a Type 0 civilization and we have not even made it onto his scale. In other words, Kardashev's scale categorizes humans in most lowly type of civilization.

There are three main types of civilizations that exist according to Nikolai Kardashev. The types have been arranged into a scale called The

Kardashev Scale, and are arranged according to how advanced they are at harnessing and utilizing energy. Additionally, others have added two extra classifications to the end of Kardashev's scale to make room for more possibilities. The types of Kardashev Civilizations are called, Type I, Type II, Type III, Type IV, and Type IV. Interestingly enough, these types of civilizations match with Thoth's descriptions of the various levels he witnessed as he travelled throughout the universe.

Here is an excerpt about the types of civilizations taken from Futurism: https://futurism.com/the-kardashev-scale-type-i-ii-iii-iv-v-civilization/

The Kardashev Scale Explained

Type I
This type of civilization consists of species who can harness energy from a neighboring star. These beings gather and store the energy from the star to provide sustenance for a growing population. Abilities these kinds of civilizations might possess would include having control over earthquakes, volcanos, and the weather. Even though these feats may be difficult for our current society to achieve, according to this scale these are just basic and primitive levels of control. It is estimated that human beings may be able to become a Type I civilization within the next hundred years.

Type II
A Type II civilization consists of beings who can actually harness the power of an entire star. This means that they can control the star and not just the energies around the star. Even in our Type I civilization, it has been hypothesized that we may be able to control a star by using a device called the Dyson Sphere. This device would be used to encompass an entire star and then gather most, if not all, of the star's energy before sending it to our planet for later use. A different method might be to create a gigantic reactor that can harness a star's energy, that is, if our race has mastered fusion power. Yet another method might involve utilizing nearby gas giants for their hydrogen.

A Type II civilization would be extremely powerful and cannot be compared to anything we currently know. If we were to become a Type II civilization, however, we would have some amazing abilities. For instance, if an object the size of our moon was on a course to crash into the earth, we could vaporize it out of existence. We could even move our planet out of the object's way! In fact, we could move another planet into its path, creating a shield that protected Earth from impact. Amazing, right?

That kind of energy could make our civilization immune to extinction.

Type III

In a Type III civilizations, their species becomes a master race. They know everything there is to know about energy. To become this type of civilization, humans would be required to go through hundreds of thousands of years of evolution, biological and mechanical. It would be reasonable to think that in future generations, when humans reach this stage, they may be much different that the humans we know and love today. These types of humans may include cyborgs, which are cybernetic beings that consist of biological and robotic body parts. Humans as we know them today may even become a sub-species in that kind of society. In all likelihood, wholly biological humans would probably be seen as inferior, unevolved, or even disabled by their cyborg counterparts.

How might this kind of civilization work? It is speculated that there might be millions of cyborgs and robots capable of self-replicating, making it possible for them to colonize entire galaxies, moving from one star to the next. If they built Dyson Spheres to encapsulate each star, then they could create a massive network to send energy back to their home planet, or other planets if needed. They would not be without perceivable complications, however, because the laws of physics would constrain them. Unless they developed a warp drive or mastered wormhole teleportation, which are only theoretical at this time, they would be limited.

Type IV

Kardeshev did not believe that a species could achieve a Type IV classification. He claimed that kind of civilization would be too advanced. Others, however, speculated that a Type IV civilization might be capable of harnessing the energy content of the entire universe, enabling them to traverse the accelerating expansion of space. These types of species might even live inside of black holes. Currently, we cannot even dare to dream of what kinds of methods this type of civilization would use to harness and generate energy.

Type V

This is where god-like beings may exist. They would have the knowledge and means of manipulating the universe as they please.

For a more detailed examination: https://www.princeton.edu/~achaney/tmve/
wiki100k/docs/Kardashev_scale.html

Humans Are Space-Born

AND THOTH SAID
Outstripping in science, they, all of the races
mighty in wisdom, sons of the stars.
Long time I paused, watching their wisdom.
Saw them create from out of the ether cities
gigantic of rose and gold.

Formed forth from the primal element,
base of all matter, the ether far flung.
Far in the past, they had conquered the ether,
Freed themselves from the bondage of toil;
ormed in their mind only a picture and swiftly
created, it grew.

Forth then, my soul sped, throughout the Cosmos,
seeing ever, new things and old;
learning that man is truly space-born,
a Sun of the Sun,
a child of the stars.

Know ye, O man, whatever from ye inhabit,
surely it is one with the stars.

Thy bodies are nothing but planets revolving
around their central suns.

When ye have gained the light of all wisdom,
free shall ye be to shine in the ether
one of the Suns that light outer darkness
one of the space-born grown into Light.

Just as the stars in time lose their brilliance,
light passing from them in to the great source,
so, O man, the soul passes onward,
leaving behind the darkness of night.
Formed forth ye, from the primal ether,
filled with the brilliance that
flows from the source,
bound by the ether coalesced around,
yet ever it flames until at last it is free.

Lift up your flame from out of the darkness,
fly from the night and ye shall be free
Traveled I through the space-time,
knowing my soul at last was set free
knowing that now might I pursue wisdom.
Until at last, I passed to a plane,
hidden from knowledge,
known not to wisdom,
extension beyond all that we know.
Now, O man, when I had this knowing,
happy my soul grew
for now I was free.
Listen, ye space-born,
list to my wisdom
know ye not that ye, too, will be free.
List ye again, O man, to my wisdom,
that hearing, ye too, might live and be free
Not of the earth are ye -- earthy,
but child of the Infinite Cosmic Light.
Know ye not, O man, of your heritage
Know ye not ye are truly the Light
Sun of the Great Sun, when ye gain wisdom,
truly aware of your kinship with Light.

Now, to ye, I give knowledge,
freedom to walk in the path I have trod

showing ye truly how by my striving,
I trod the path that leads to the stars.

Hark ye, O man, and know of thy bondage,
know how to free thyself from the toils.
Out of the darkness shall ye rise upward,
one with the Light and one with the stars.
Follow ye ever the path of wisdom.
Only by this can ye rise from below.

Ever man's destiny leads him onwar
into the Curves of Infinity's ALL.

Know ye, O man, that all space is ordered.
Only by Order are ye One with the ALL.

Order and Balance are the Law of the Cosmos.
Follow and ye shall be One with the ALL.

He who would follow the pathway of wisdom,
open must be he to the flower of life,
extending his consciousness out of the darkness,
flowing through time and space in the ALL.

....."Learning that man is truly space-born..." Meaning we are children of an alien race. Thoth is saying that we are made of Atoms. Our bodies are nothing but planets revolving

Thoth has made another direct reference to syncing (synchronizing) with the Universal Consciousness in order to obtain knowledge and wisdom.

AND THOTH SAID
Deep in the silence,
first ye must linger until at last ye
are free from desire,
free from the longing to speak in the silence.
Conquer by silence, the bondage of words.

Abstaining from eating until we have conquered
desire for food, that is bondage of soul.
Then lie ye down in the darkness.
Close ye your eyes from the rays of the Light.
Centre thy soul-force in the place of thine consciousness,
shaking it free from the bonds of the night.

Place in thy mind-place the image thou desireth.
Picture the place thou desireth to see.
Vibrate back and forth with thy power.
Loosen the soul from out of its night.

Fiercely must thou shake with all of thy power
until at last thy soul shall be free.

Mighty beyond words is the flame of the Cosmic,
hanging in planes, unknown to man;
mighty and balanced, moving in Order,
music of harmonies, far beyond man.

Speaking with music, singing with color,
flame from the beginning of Eternity's ALL.

Spark of the flame art thou, O my children,
burning with color and living with music.
List to the voice and thou shalt be free.

Consciousness free is fused with the Cosmic,
One with the Order and Law of the ALL.

Knew ye not man, that out of the darkness,
Light shall flame forth, a symbol of ALL.

Pray ye this prayer for attaining of wisdom.
Pray for the coming of Light to the ALL.

Mighty SPIRIT of LIGHT that shines through the
Cosmos, draw my flame closer in harmony to thee.

Lift up my fire from out of the darkness,
magnet of fire that is One with the ALL.

Lift up my soul, thou mighty and potent.
Child of the Light, turn not away.
Draw me in power to melt in thy furnace;
One with all things and all things
in One, fire of the life-strain and
One with the Brain.

When ye have freed thy soul from its bondage,
know that for ye the darkness is gone.
Ever through space ye may seek wisdom,
bound not be fetters forged in the flesh.

Onward and upward into the morning, free flash,
O Soul, to the realms of Light. Move thou in Order,
move thou in Harmony, freely shalt move
with the Children of Light.

Seek ye and know ye, my KEY of Wisdom.
Thus, O man, ye shall surely be free.

CHAPTER SEVEN

The Dweller Of Unal

Emerald Tablet Five

AND THOTH SAID
Oft dream I of buried Atlantis,
lost in the ages that have passed into night.
Aeon on aeon thou existed in beauty,
a light shining through the darkness of night.
Mighty in power, ruling the earth-born,
Lord of the Earth in Atlantis' day.

This reference to a sunken and lost Atlantis confirms Plato's account of a sunken Atlantean city. Atlantis was a global civilization.

AND THOTH SAID
King of the nations, master of wisdom,
LIGHT through SUNTAL,
Keeper of the way,
dwelt in his TEMPLE,
the MASTER of UNAL,

LIGHT of the Earth in Atlantis' day.

Master, HE, from a cycle beyond us,
living in bodies as one among men."
Not as the earth-born,
HE from beyond us,
SUN of a cycle, advanced beyond men.
Know ye, O man, that HORLET the Master,
was never one with the children of men.

According to Thoth, they grow cloned avatar bodies and transfer their consciousness into them.

AND THOTH SAID

Far in the past time when Atlantis first grew as a power,
appeared there one with the KEY of WISDOM,
showing the way of LIGHT to all.

Showed he to all men the path of attainment,
way of the Light that flows among men.
Mastering darkness, leading the MAN-SOUL,
upward to heights that were One with the Light.
Divided the Kingdoms, HE into sections.
Ten were they, ruled by children of men.

Upon another, built HE a TEMPLE,
built but not by the children of men.

Out of the ETHER called HE its substance,
molded and formed by the power of YTOLAN
into the forms HE built with His mind.

Mile upon mile it covered the island,
space upon space it grew in its might.
Black, yet not black, but dark like the space-time,
deep in its heart the ESSENCE of LIGHT.

Swiftly the TEMPLE grew into being,
molded and shaped by the WORD of the DWELLER,
called from the formless into a form.

Thoth is talking about using vocal frequency and vibration to call matter into existence. This may sound like science fiction, but we have already began to duplicate this in what we call modern laboratories. Scientists have already discovered how to turn light into matter.

To learn more about their eight-year quest, check out this article:
https://phys.org/news/2014-05-scientists-year-quest.html

AND THOTH SAID

Builded HE then, within it, great chambers,
filled them with forms called forth from the ETHER,
filled them with wisdom called forth by His mind.
Formless was HE within his TEMPLE,
yet was HE formed in the image of men.

Dwelling among them yet not of them,
strange and far different
was HE from the children of men.
Chose HE then from among the people,
THREE who became his gateway.

Choose HE the THREE from the Highest
to become his links with Atlantis.

Messengers they, who carried his council,
to the kings of the children of men.

Brought HE forth others and taught them wisdom;
teachers, they, to the children of men.
Placed HE them on the island of UNDAL to stand as
teachers of LIGHT to men.

Each of those who were thus chosen,
taught must he be for years five and ten.

Only thus could he have understanding to bring
LIGHT to the children of men.

Thus there came into being the Temple, a dwelling place
for the Master of men.
I, THOTH, have ever sought wisdom,

searching in darkness and searching in Light.

Long in my youth I traveled the pathway,
seeking ever new knowledge to gain.

Until after much striving, one of the THREE,
to me brought the LIGHT.
Brought HE to me the commands of the DWELLER,
called me from the darkness into the LIGHT.

Brought HE me, before the DWELLER,
deep in the Temple before the great FIRE.

There on the great throne, beheld I,
the DWELLER, clothed with the LIGHT
and flashing with fire.
Down I knelt before that great wisdom,
feeling the LIGHT flowing through me in waves.

Heard I then the voice of the DWELLER:
'O darkness, come into the Light.

Long have ye sought the pathway to light.

Each soul on earth that loosens its fetters,
shall soon be made free from the bondage of night.

Forth from the darkness have ye arisen,
closer approached the Light of your goal.

Here ye shall dwell as one of my children,
keeper of records gathered by wisdom,
instrument thou of the LIGHT from beyond.

Ready by thou made to do what is needed,
preserver of wisdom through the ages of darkness,
that shall come fast on the children of men.

'Live thee here and drink of all wisdom.
Secrets and mysteries unto thee shall unveil.'

Then answered I, the MASTER OF CYCLES, saying:
'O Light, that descended to men,
give thou to me of thy wisdom that
I might be a teacher of men.
Give thou of thy LIGHT that I may be free.'

Spoke then to me again, the MASTER:
'Age after age shall ye live through
your wisdom, Aye, when o'er Atlantis the ocean waves roll,
holding the Light, though hidden in darkness,
ready to come when e'er thou shalt call.
Go thee now and learn greater wisdom.
Grow thou through LIGHT to Infinity's ALL.'

Long then dwelt I in the Temple of the DWELLER
until at last I was One with the LIGHT.
Followed I then the path to the star planes,
followed I then the pathway to LIGHT.
Deep into Earth's heart I followed the pathway,
learning the secrets, below as above;
learning the pathway to the HALLS of AMENTI;
learning the LAW that balances the world.

To Earth's hidden chambers pierced I by my wisdom,
deep through the Earth's crust, into the pathway,
hidden for ages from the children of men.
Unveiled before me, ever more wisdom until
I reached a new knowledge: found that all is part of an ALL,
great and yet greater than all that we know.
Searched I Infinity's heart through all the ages.
Deep and yet deeper, more mysteries I found.
Now, as I look back through the ages,
know I that wisdom is boundless,

ever grown greater throughout the ages,
One with Infinity's greater than all.
Light there was in ancient ATLANTIS.
Yet, darkness, too, was hidden in all.

Fell from the Light into the darkness,
some who had risen to heights among men.

Proud they became because of their knowledge,
proud were they of their place among men.
Deep delved they into the forbidden,
opened the gateway that led to below.

Sought they to gain ever more knowledge but
seeking to bring it up from below.
He who descends below must have balance,
else he is bound by lack of our Light.

Opened, they then,
by their knowledge,
pathways forbidden to man.

But, in His Temple, all-seeing, the DWELLER,
lay in his AGWANTI, while through Atlantis,
His soul roamed free.

Saw HE the Atlanteans, by their magic,
opening the gateway that would
bring to Earth a great woe.

Fast fled His soul then, back to His body.
Up HE arose from His AGWANTI.
Called HE the Three mighty messengers.
Gave the commands that shattered the world.
Deep 'neath Earth's crust to the HALLS of AMENTI,
swiftly descended the DWELLER.

Called HE then on the powers the Seven Lords wielded;
changed the Earth's balance.

Down sank Atlantis beneath the dark waves.
Shattered the gateway that had been opened;
shattered the doorway that led down below.
All of the islands were shattered except UNAL,
and part of the island of the sons of the DWELLER.

Preserved HE them to be the teachers,
Lights on the path for those to come after,
Lights for the lesser children of men.

Called HE then, I THOTH, before him,
gave me commands for all I should do, saying;
Take thou, O THOTH, all of your wisdom.
Take all your records, Take all your magic.
Go thou forth as a teacher of men.
Go thou forth reserving the records
until in time LIGHT grows among men.
LIGHT shalt thou be all through the ages,
hidden yet found by enlightened men.
Over all Earth, give we ye power,
free thou to give or take it away.

Gather thou now the sons of Atlantis.
Take them and flee to the people of the rock caves.
Fly to the land of the Children of KHEM."
Then gathered I the sons of Atlantis.
Into the spaceship I brought all my records,
brought the records of sunken Atlantis.
Gathered I all of my powers,
instruments many of mighty magic.

Up then we rose on wings of the morning.
High we arose above the Temple,

leaving behind the Three and DWELLER,
deep in the HALLS 'neath the Temple,
closing the pathway to the LORDS of the Cycles.

Yet ever to him who has knowing,
open shall be the path to AMENTI.
Fast fled we then on the wings of the morning,
fled to the land of the children of KHEM.
There by my power,
I conquered and ruled them.

Raised I to LIGHT,
the children of KHEM.
Deep 'neath the rocks,
I buried my spaceship,
waiting the time when man might be free.

Over the spaceship,
erected a marker in the form
of a lion yet like unto man.
There 'neath the image rests yet my spaceship,
forth to be brought when need shall arise.

Know ye, O man, that far in the future,
invaders shall come from out of the deep.
Then awake, ye who have wisdom.
Bring forth my ship and conquer with ease.
Deep 'neath the image lies my secret.
Search and find in the pyramid I built.

Each to the other is the Keystone;
each the gateway that leads into LIFE.
Follow the KEY I leave behind me.
Seek and the doorway to LIFE shall be thine.
Seek thou in my pyramid,

deep in the passage that ends in a wall.

Use thou the KEY of the SEVEN,
and open to thee the pathway will fall.
Now unto thee I have given my wisdom.
Now unto thee I have given my way.

Follow the pathway.
Solve thou my secrets.
Unto thee I have shown the way.

The esoteric message in tablet five is that "the only way out, is in." We must all take a journey to inner space. According to Thoth, only then can we truly synchronize with the Universal Consciousness and break free from the illusion of the physical realm.

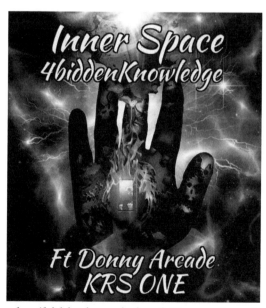

Inner Space by 4biddenknowledge ft Donny Arcade and KRS-ONE
Now Available On All Music Stores.

CHAPTER EIGHT

THE KEY OF MAGIC

Emerald Tablet Six

In tablet Six, Thoth exposes the fact that dark forces were already at work before he arrived on Earth. A real battle between dark and light using magic spells to control the fate of the existing beings that were already here evolving on earth. This epic tablet covers the power of uttered words backed by intent and how the resulting frequency can have a direct effect on the ether of spacetime itself. You have the power to alter the events inside your reality tunnel.

AND THOTH SAID
Hark ye, O man, to the wisdom of magic.
Hark the knowledge of powers forgotten.
Long ago in the days of the first man,
warfare began between darkness and light.

Men then as now,
were filled with both darkness and light;
and while in some darkness held sway,
in other light filled the soul.

Aye, age old in this warfare,
the eternal struggle between darkness and light.
Fiercely is it fought all through the ages,
using strange powers hidden to man.

Adepts has there been filled with the blackness,
struggling always against the light;
but others there are who, filled with brightness,
have ever conquered the darkness of night.

Where e'er ye may be in all ages and plane,
surely, ye shall know of the battle with night.

Long ages ago,
The SUNS of the Morning
descending, found the world filled with night,
there in that past, began the struggle,
the age old Battle Darkness & Light.

An Adept is a person who is skilled or proficient at something.

AND THOTH SAID

Many in the time were so filled with darkness
that only feebly flamed the light from the night.
Some they were, masters of darkness,
who sought to fill all with their darkness:
Sought to draw others into their night.

Fiercely withstood they, the masters of brightness:
fiercely fought they from the darkness of night
Sought ever to tighten the fetters,
the chains that bind men to the darkness of night.

Used they always the dark magic,
brought into men by the power of darkness.
magic that enshrouded man's soul with darkness.

Could these verses be the original source of the yin and yang concept?

The theory of yin and yang is much more complicated than most people realize. Many believe it's simply a comparison of opposites, yet the yin yang theory explains our dualistic universe.

There are four main aspects of yin and yang.

Aspect 1: Yin and Yang are Opposites

This is the most popular aspect of yin and yang and people easily understand the basics of this aspect. What they might not realize, however, is that the opposition of yin and yang is relative. For instance, Spring is yin when compared to Summer, but it is yang when compared to Winter. Yin and yang are never static but ever changing while maintaining balance. Here is something else you may find fascinating about the seasons and how they relate to yin and yang: Summer is known as the season that is yang within yang, while Winter is known as the season that is yin within yin. Likewise, Autumn is the season of yang within yin, while Spring is the season of yin within yang.

Aspect 2: Yin and Yang are Interdependent

This means that yin cannot exist without yang, and yang cannot exist without yin. Their very existence depends on each other. Additionally, nothing is completely yin or completely yang. As demonstrated in the yin-yang symbol, each contains an aspect of the other. For example, night cannot exist without day, and day cannot exist without night. Classic Asian literature states that yin creates yang and yang activates yin.

Aspect 3: Yin and Yang Mutually Consume Each Other

This means that when yin or yang become imbalanced, they affect and can weaken each other. Relative levels of yin and yang change constantly, and these changes are typically harmonious. If one gets too strong or too weak, however, it will imbalance the other. For example, if you place an ice cube (yin) into a cup of hot water (yang), the water becomes warm as it consumes the ice, causing each of them to lose their original state of being intensely yin or yang.

Aspect 4: Yin and Yang Can Transform Into Each Other

Because the relationship between yin and yang is dynamic, they can transform into each other. The transformation is never random and can only occur at the right moment. An example of how yin can transform into yang exists in the example I used above when speaking about the seasons. Winter, a yin season, transforms into Spring, a yang season in comparison, at the right time of year.

The principle of yin and yang dates back to the 3rd century BCE or even earlier. It is a fundamental concept in Chinese philosophy and culture. A cosmologist named Zou Yen (or Tsou Yen) helped make the concept popular when he theorized that life went through the five phases of fire, water, metal, wood, and earth, which continually interchanged according to the principles of yin and yang.

To give you a better understanding of yin and yang, I will list the most common attributes below.

Attributes of Yin:

- Gender: feminine

- Color: black

- Quality: dark

- Direction: North

- Element: Water

- Activity: Passive

- Movement: Still

- Inner Sense: Intuition

- Phase: Earth

- Planet: Moon

- Temperature: Cold

- Age: Old

- Numerology: Even numbers

- Topography: Valleys

- Status: Poor

- Texture: Soft

- Qualities: Yin is the spirit of all things. It is the creative, downward seeking, and submissive. During the course of a day, it reaches its height at 4:00am and over the course of a year, it is highest at the winter solstice (In the Northern Hemisphere).

Attributes of Yang:

- Gender: masculine

- Color: white

- Quality: light
- Direction: South
- Element: Fire
- Activity: Active
- Movement: Moving
- Inner Sense: Logic
- Phase: Fire
- Planet: Sun
- Temperature: Hot
- Age: Young
- Numerology: Odd numbers
- Topography: Mountains
- Status: Rich
- Texture: Hard
- Qualities: Yang is the energy of all things. It is the enlightening, strong, dominant and creation itself. downward seeking, and submissive. During the course of a day, it reaches its height at 12:00pm and over the course of a year, it is highest at the summer solstice (In the Northern Hemisphere).

If you want to learn more about yin and yang, I recommend this website:

https://www.ancient.eu/Yin_and_Yang/

AND THOTH SAID
Banded together as in order,
Brothers of Darkness,
they through the ages,
antagonist they to the children of men.
Walked they always secret and hidden,
found, yet not found by the children of men.

Forever, they walked and worked in darkness,

hiding from the light in the darkness of night.
Silently, secretly use they their power,
enslaving and binding the soul of men...

Dark is the way of the Dark Brothers travel,
dark of the darkness not of the night,
traveling o'er Earth
they walk through man's dreams.
Power they have gained
from the darkness around them
to call other dwellers from out of their plane,
in ways that are dark and unseen by man.
Into man's mind-space reach the Dark Brothers...

Mighty are they in the forbidden knowledge
forbidden because it is one with the night.

Surrender not your soul to the Brothers of Darkness.
Keep thy face ever turned towards the Light...

List ye, O man, to he who comes to you.
But weigh in the balance if his words be of light.
For many there are who walk in Dark Brightness
and yet are not the children of light.

When one looks at the current state of the world today, one can clearly
see that the world is led by the "Dark Brothers." These days we call them
Secret Societies with elitist agendas. With their control over countries,
corporations, military, and media, they get into "man's mind space" as
Thoth so eloquently stated above.

AND THOTH SAID
Now I give unto thee the knowledge,
known to the Masters,
the knowing that conquers all the dark fears.
Use this, the wisdom I give thee.

Master thou shalt be of The Brothers of Night.

When unto thee comes a feeling,
drawing thee nearer to the darker gate,
examine thine heart and find if the feeling
thou hast has come from within.
If thou shalt find the darkness thine own thoughts,
banish them forth from the place in thy mind.

Send through thy body a wave of vibration,
irregular first and regular second,
repeating time after time until free.
Start the WAVE FORCE in thy BRAIN CENTER.
Direct it in waves from thine head to thy foot.

But if thou findest thine heart is not darkened,
be sure that a force is directed to thee.
Only by knowing can thou overcome it.
Only be wisdom can thou hope to be free.
Knowledge brings wisdom and wisdom is power.
Attain and ye shall have power o'er all.

Seek ye first a place bound by darkness.
Place ye a circle around about thee.
Stand erect in the midst of the circle.
Use thou this formula, and you shalt be free.
Raise thou thine hands to the dark space above thee.

Close thou thine eyes and draw in the LIGHT."
Thoth gives specific instructions on what to do in order to
discover the light of knowledge and universal consciousness.

Call to the SPIRIT OF LIGHT through the Space-Time,
using these words and thou shalt be free:
Fill thou my body, O SPIRIT OF LIfe,
'fill thou my body with SPIRIT OF LIGHT.

Come from the FLOWER
that shines through the darkness.
Come from the HALLS where the Seven Lords rule.'

These Seven Lords represent the Seven Chakra systems in the body. Each is tuned to a specific frequency. To learn them is to find a way to power over one's limitations of consciousness.

Study these Seven Chakras in order to develop an enabling spirit that will guide you to higher levels of consciousness and knowledge.

Root Chakra
The Root Chakra is located in the midline at the base of the spine, in the tailbone area, and represents our foundational feelings of being grounded and supported. Issues in this chakra often relate to survival and focus on food, shelter, and money.

Sacral Chakra
The Sacral Chakra is located in the midline of the lower abdomen, roughly two inches below the navel and two inches interior to the skin. Issues in this chakra often relate to a sense of abundance, well-being, creativity, pleasure, and sexuality.

Solar Plexus Chakra
The Solar Plexus Chakra is located in the midline above the belly button and just below the sternum. This chakra often relates to will power, control, and anything to do with the idea and conviction of the self. Therefore, issues with self-worth, self-confidence, and self-esteem often arise when the Solar Plexus Chakra is out of balance.

Heart Charka
The Heart Chakra is located in the midline just above the heart. This chakra affects our ability to love, experience joy, and find inner peace.

Throat Chakra
The Throat Chakra is located in the middle of the throat. This chakra affects our self-expression related to feelings and truth.

Third Eye Chakra

The Third Eye Chakra is located on the forehead and between the eyebrows. This chakra affects our intuition, imagination, wisdom, and our ability to think and make sound decisions.

Crown Chakra

The Crown Chakra is located at highest point of the head. It allows us to connect with our spiritual natures and higher energies. Emotions related to this chakra include feelings about inner and outer beauty and bliss.

To learn more about the chakras, check out this article:

https://blog.mindvalley.com/7-chakras/

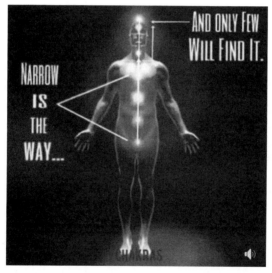

Image courtesy of Pantheon Elite Records – 7 Chakras by Donny Arcade

The following statement reveals the most important lesson in the Thoth tablets. Perhaps, it is the most important lesson in this entire book.

Frequency and vibration have a direct effect on our reality and can even alter current and future events.

Thoth tells the reader to speak the following names aloud:

UNTANAS
QUERTAS
CHIETAL,
GOYANA
HUERTAL
SEMVETA
ARDAL

These names are not the names of real people. They are frequencies that when spoken aloud, send out specific vibrational frequencies that have a direct effect on our brain which in turn, have an effect on your personal reality tunnel.

Thoth instructs that you are to use this technique as needed. Meaning that there is not a permanent long-lasting effect, but that the effect may be temporary and may need to be repeated as needed.

Those influenced later by Thoth (if not incarnate by Thoth), no less than Pythagoras and Newton, discovered how to acquiesce the power of vibrational knowledge.

Iamblichus wrote that Pythagoras "extended his ears and fixed his intellect in the sublime symphonies of the world, he alone hearing and understanding, as it appears, the universal harmony and consonance of the spheres and the stars that are moved through them and which produce a fuller and more intense melody than anything affected by mortal sounds...And he called the medicine which is obtained through music by the name of purification." *The Life of Pythagoras*, by Thomas Taylor.

Newton experienced an ethereal plane (also known as the astral plane)--a ubiquitous supple material lighter than air, providing a pathway for receiving vibrations.

AND THOTH SAID
By their names I call them to aid me,
free me and save me from the darkness of night:
UNTANAS, QUERTAS, CHIETAL,
and GOYANA, HUERTAL, SEMVETA--ARDAL.
By their names I implore thee,
free me from darkness

and fill me with LIGHT.

See ye not that the names have the power
to free by vibration the fetters that bind?
Use them at need to free thou thine brother
so that he, too, may come forth from the night.

In these passages, Thoth instructs that by calling aloud the names of the Seven Lords, that the power of vibrations will empower the believer to be free from the powers that prohibit him from the attainment of knowledge through higher consciousness.

Image Credit 4biddenknowledge

The Mozart effect on seizures

The music of Mozart is the subject of intense scrutiny to see if it has other properties. The April 2001 edition of "Journal of the Royal Society of Medicine," assessed the possible health benefits of the music of Mozart. "John Jenkins played Sonata K448 to patients with epilepsy and found a decrease in epileptiform activity. The research looked at twenty-nine people with severe epilepsy. Their brainwaves were measured as they listened to the music and twenty-three people showed reduced epileptic activity. In one patient, the epileptic activity dropped from being present two thirds of the time, to just one fifth of the time. In two other patients, who experience epileptic activity ninety percent of the time, this dropped to fifty percent. Whatever the effect of the music is, it isn't simply related to enjoying the music, because many of the people were asleep during these tests. The effect stopped when the music stopped, so in order to assess the longer term effect, an eight year old girl was played music for 10 minutes in every hour. Her seizures fell from nine in the first hour to one in the last hour. On the second day she had just two seizures in eight hours. Professor John Jenkins from the University of London, author of the paper "The Mozart Effect" thinks the music in some way affects the electrical impulses of the brain." https://www.epilepsyqueensland.com.au/mozart-effect

Cymatics

Is matter affected by outside influences? The study of cymatics, as well as how frequencies help to create what we perceive as matter, expands our understanding of such possible connections. Cymatics is the study of sound and vibration made visible, typically on the surface of a plate, diaphragm or membrane.

Cymatics History

"The provenance of Cymatics is traceable at least 1000 years ago to African tribes who used the taut skin of drums sprinkled with small grains to divine future events. The drum is one of oldest known musical instruments and the effects of sand on a vibrating drumhead have probably been known for millennia." The History of Musical Instruments, by Curt Sachs.

Leonardo Da Vinci

Leonardo Da Vinci noticed that vibrating a wooden table on which dust lay created various shapes. "I say then that when a table is struck in different places the dust that is upon it is reduced to various shapes of mounds and tiny hillocks. The dust descends from the hypotenuse of these hillocks, enters beneath their base and raises itself again around the axis of the point of the hillock." Notebooks of Leonardo da Vinci, by Curdy E. Mac.

Galileo Galilei

"Galileo Galilei described scraping a brass plate with a chisel and noticed a "long row of fine streaks, parallel and equidistant from one another," presumably caused by the brass filings dancing on the surface of the plate and finding safe haven in a series of parallel nodal striations."

Traits of Physics by J. B. Biot.

Robert Hooke

Robert Hooke was an English scientist of Oxford University who contributed to many scientific fields including mathematics, optics, mechanics and astronomy. Hook devised a simple apparatus in 1680 consisting of a glass plate covered with flour that he induced a response with a violin bow. It is not known whether Hooke had access to the notebooks of Leonardo da Vinci or Galileo or if he devised the apparatus independently.

Ernst Chladni

A German musician and scientist, Ernst Chladni is sometimes called "the father of acoustics." Even though he had access to Hooke's work, Chladni is the the one history decided to acknowledge for his study of this class of phenomena. Chladni utilized a sand-strewn brass plate, which was excited by a violin bow. He found that he was able to create a large number of archetypal geometric patterns, which came to be known as "Chladni Figures."

From Chladni's pioneering book, *Discoveries in the Theory of Sound,* we learn that Chladni demonstrated this seemingly magical phenomenon all over Europe and even had an audience with Napoleon. The French leader was so impressed he sponsored a competition with The French Academy of Sciences to acquire a mathematical explanation of the sand patterns. Sophie Germain, a young French woman, won Napoleon's 3,000 Franc prize in 1816. She wrote a mathematical explanation involving wave-like functions to describe how sound created the geometric patterns. The inference was that sound waves were responsible for creating areas of vibration and areas of stillness on the surface of the plate. It was believed that the crest of the sound 'wave's caused certain areas of the plate to vibrate while the corresponding troughs caused other areas to remain still. The sand gathered in the still areas is considered an important milestone in launching the science of acoustics.

The term "wave" has historically been used to describe sound even though it is a misnomer since sound does not, in fact, travel in waves. Sound propagates spherically or in beams, depending upon frequency. For example, at frequencies audible to humans, 20 Hertz to 20,000 Hertz, the sonic envelope is almost perfectly spherical in its form whereas at frequencies audible to bats and dolphins, above 100,000 Hertz, sound propagates in searchlight-like beams, the beam angle being dependent on frequency. Higher frequencies cause a reduction in beam angle.

This information is accredited to *What is Cymatics,* by John Stuart and Annalise Shandra Reid.

Michael Faraday

Michael Faraday, the English chemist and physicist, studied what he termed "crispations" (contractions or curling effects). His diary records many experiments in which he studied the effects of vibration on water, oil and fine grains. Faraday was fascinated by these phenomena and always sensible of good demonstrations to his audiences at the Royal Institution. *Faraday, The Life* by James Hamilton.

Faraday discovered that after putting a candle exactly below a plate and holding a screen of tracing paper an inch above it, the picture given was beautiful. Each heap of sand gave a sliver (Ã¢â‚¬Ëœstar) of light at its focus, which twinkled, appeared and disappeared with the heap continually as it rose and fell. At the corners, a fainter light appeared, and then as the screen was nearer or farther lines of light in two or even four directions appeared constant. This was a brilliant spectacle easily visible to a large audience. Faraday discovered the first physical phenomenon linking light and magnetism. *Faraday Rotation,* by Kishore Padmaraju.

John William Strutt (Lord Rayleigh)

John William Strutt (Lord Rayleigh) was an English physicist Strutt earned the Nobel Prize for Physics. He discovered surface waves in seismology, now known as Rayleigh waves. His major work, *Theory of Sound, Volumes I and II*, includes research on the 'Vibrations of Plates' and is still considered an important work. In it, he explored modal phenomena in depth, now part of the emergent science of cymatics

Margaret Watts

Margaret Watts-Hughes lived in Wales and experimented with a device she invented in 1885, which she named the "Eidophone." The eidophone was comprised of a wooden resonating chamber which opened to an end covered by a rubber membrane. That rubber membrane was strewn with sand and other media. She would sing into a tube that was connected with the resonating chamber, which created patterns and figures by using her voice.

People speculate that she may have been influenced by Michael Faraday's work because, like him, she called her patterns, "crispations."

Like Faraday she was enamored by beauty of the figures related them to her realty in an article she wrote that stated, "I have gone on singing into shape these peculiar forms, and stepping out of doors, have seen their parallels in the flowers, ferns, and trees around me; and again, as I have watched the little heaps in the formation of the floral figures gather themselves up and then shoot out their petals, just as a flower springs from the swollen bud the hope has come to me that these humble experiments may afford some suggestions in regard to nature's production of her own beautiful forms." *The Eidophone Voice Figures,* by Margaret Watts-Hughes.

Mary Desiree

Mary Desiree Waller was Professor of Physics at the Royal Free Hospital Medical School in London. She became fascinated by Chladni's work and recreated all the forms he discovered, taking his work to a higher level. Her book, *Chladni Figures, a Study in Symmetry,* includes details of her novel method of exciting plates employing solid carbon dioxide chips. She approached the subject of Chladni Figures with scientific rigor and her work represents a rich resource for students of this branch of acoustics, including some of the mathematical equations that describe the phenomena.

Hans Jenny

Cymatics comes from Greek, meaning wave or billow in describing the periodic effects that sound and vibration has on matter. The term was coined by Hans Jenny, a Swiss medical doctor and pioneer of the philosophical school known as anthroposophy. The generic term for this field of science is the study of "modal phenomena-Cymatics." *Cymatics: Volume I*, by Hans Jenny. His two volumes are rich sources of cymatic imagery, which he observed and described in great detail, although leaving scientific and mathematical explanations to scientists who would come after him. Jenny invented the "Tonoscope" a device similar to Watts-Hughes' Eidophone, but including an electro-mechanical transducer to excite the membrane. He was also the first to suggest that such a device may one day assist deaf individuals to acquire speech. Jenny also excited steel plates using piezo crystal elements driven by an electronic oscillator, devices not available to Watts-Hughes and other acoustic pioneers of the past. The piezo crystal transducers were able to excite the plates in a wide range of frequencies, including high audible frequencies, resulting in the formation of complex sand-pattern forms.

Alexander Lauterwasser

Alexander Lauterwasser is a German researcher and photographer basing his work on that of Hans Jenny. Lauterwasser is interested in the phenomenology and typography of the shapes formed by the effects of sound on water and in comparing the shapes with those that occur in nature, such as in the morphogenesis of creatures and the archetypal forms of inanimate matter. His 2002 book, *Water Sound Images,* set new standards in cymatic imagery.

Thomas J. Mitchell

Thomas J. Mitchell is a Scottish musician who studied the ornately carved ceiling of Rosslyn Chapel for twenty-seven years. Rosslyn Chapel, near Edinburgh, famous for its lavish carvings and its association with the Knights Templar, also contained a mystery in the form of four sections of arches containing cymatic-like designs carved into the faces of 215 rectilinear cubes.Mitchell discovered that the patterns related to musical notes, to be read in a specific order, postulating that the builders of the chapel had access to Chladni-style plate and bow technology and deliberately encoded the melody into the cubes. His son, Stuart Mitchell, orchestrated the music thus revealed, and named it 'The Rosslyn Motet.' It was played on traditional medieval musical instruments in the chapel in September 2006. Mitchell"s book, *Rosslyn Chapel:The Music of the Cubes,* is my source for this information.

John Stuart Reid

John Stuart Reid is an acoustics engineer who carried out cymatics research in the King's Chamber of the Great Pyramid of Egypt in 1997. Reid published his research results in Egyptian Sonics, seventeen containing photographs of the cymatic patterns that formed on a PVC (polyvinyl chloride) membrane he stretched over the sarcophagus. The experiment was designed to study the resonant behavior of the granite from which the sarcophagus is fashioned. Since many of the images strongly resemble ancient Egyptian hieroglyphs, Reid postulated that the inherent resonances of granite, when radiated as a complex sound field during the crafting of the stone, might have influenced the development of hieroglyphic writing. Reid subsequently began experimenting with instrumentation that would enable an accurate visual equivalent of sound to be created from any audible sound, resulting in the invention of the CymaScope. Reid worked with American design engineer, Erik Larson to engineer the instrument to Pythagorean proportions.

Reid recognized that the wave model of sound is incomplete because it does not characterize the spherical space-form of audible sound. CymaGlyph images, created on the CymaScope, are considered to be analogs of sound and music since the geometries they contain represent mathematical correlates of the musical pitches that caused the pattern to form on the instrument's membrane.One of the many potential applications being explored for the CymaScope is the decipherment of dolphin language in collaboration with SpeakDolphin.com, a Florida-based organization formed for this purpose. *Sonic Age*, by John Reid is quoted above for this information. Many resources for the study of Reid's work can be found at: http://www.cymascope.com

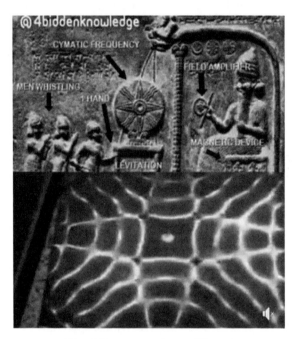

Visual Representations of Sound

Secrets of the Anunnaki explained by modern science

The Anunnaki of ancient Sumer and contemporaries of the earliest Egyptian dynasties, taught humans the secrets of levitation or antigravity. You can see this Anunnaki giant in above Sumerian cylinder scroll that has been analyzed dozens of times by scholars, but the secret eludes them. How are we to look at this? Scientifically speaking, four things are necessary to reverse the magnetic polarity in an object.

1. Magnetic field generator. The Anunnaki king is sitting on that device. Notice the Lions on the box facing opposite each other. That represents the opposing magnetic fields.

2. Field Amplifier. That's the technology device in the Anunnaki kings hand. He uses that to control and modulate the magnetic field.

3. Cymatic frequency generator. The cymatics are the most important. You must place the cymatic frequency directly on top of the object that you want to levitate. You can generate a cymatic frequency using a home stereo speaker and amp. Research cymatics in your free time.

4. A loud whistle. Notice the two men whistling behind the man lifting the stone table with one hand. The whistling tone interacts with the magnetic field and the cymatic frequency and the atoms in the stone table reverse polarity greatly reducing the tables gravitational field. https://astrologymemes.com/i/q4biddenknowledge-cymatic-frequency-amplih-men-whistling-i-han-now-wait-14092837

If you have been following my page for a while, you would have seen a post that I made about my visit to the Coral Castle in Miami Florida. It was built in modern times by a 4'11" man named Edward Leedskalnin. He claimed to have rediscovered the secrets of ancient Egyptian stone building and Stone levitation. He worked alone and could often be heard whistling. Edward used a very similar device as shown above in this post. All matter in the 3rd Dimension can be completely manipulated because matter is only a frequency condensed into a slower vibration. Everything is vibration, sound and frequency emanating from electromagnetic waves. In the beginning was the Word (which equals) Frequency and vibration. Let That 4biddenknowledge Marinate!

Now that we did an extensive review of how frequencies help to create our reality. Let's look at how "words" backed by conscious intent also have a direct effect on the world around us.

The power of words and thoughts were connected to the power of human consciousness by Professor Masaru Emoto of Japan in this century. He researched the physical effects of words, prayer, and music on the crystalline structure of water. Water that was exposed to positive intentions like love and gratitude have crystalline structures far more balanced and pleasing than water exposed to dark and negative phrases. His research on the power of consciousness to control the molecular structure of water is significant, forcing us to realize that it is possible for our thoughts to influence human beings, since humans are as a whole almost sixty-five percent water. Furthermore, our hearts and brains are seventy-three percent water, and our lungs are eighty-three percent water. Controlling our heart rhythms created a more sustained blood pressure level. If our brains are the seat of our consciousness, then ought we not be better equipped to develop higher levels of consciousness? Regular breathing through our lungs guarantees successful meditation, thus bringing us closer to our own inner balance.

Forzen Water Crystals

Dr. Masaru Emoto's work illustrates that by the power of our own introspection we are capable of altering our understanding and acceptance of our world. His research provides the evidence that we can positively influence ourselves and everything around us simply by selecting words of power. http://www.masaru-emoto.net/english/water-crystal.html

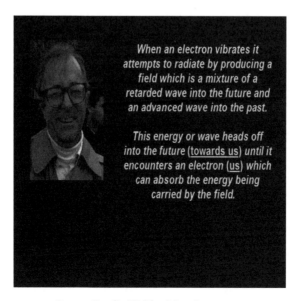

Image Credit HiddenMeanings.com

•Radiation generally means the transmission of waves, objects or information from a source into a surrounding medium or destination.
en.wikipedia.org/wiki/Radiation

LIGHT: Electromagnetic radiation of any wavelength.

1 John 1:5. This then is the message which we have heard of him, and declare unto you, that God is light

Image Credit HiddenMeanings.com

CHAPTER NINE

THE SEVEN LORDS

Emerald Tablet Seven

The masters of the cycles are working in correlation to the cyclical cycles of the rise and fall of civilizations as well as the rise and fall of humankind's energetic light being. Thoth is telling humanity that he is headed towards a higher frequency shift that will allow him to reach higher dimensions of consciousness. There are dark forces that seek to keep humankind at a lower material frequency. The Seven Lords also represent the established Seven Chakra centers that were set up to allow humankind to reach higher realms of consciousness.

4biddenknowledge

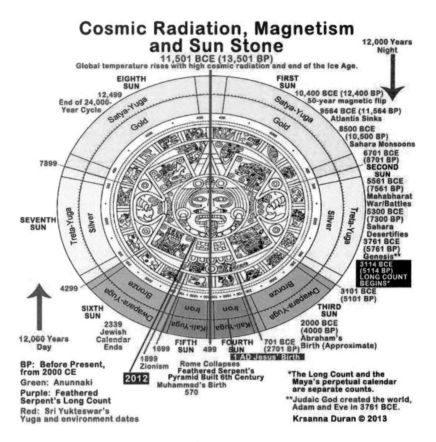

Image Credit Krsanna Duran

Knowledge of Hare-Krishna

In the incarnations of Krsna appear, "There are four ages (Yugas) for acquiring knowledge, gold, silver, bronze, and hypocrisy. I encourage you to read about these four ages in your quest to learn all manifestations of acquiring knowledge and consciousness." Research more about this from this site: http://www.harekrishnatemple.com/chapter19.html

AND THOTH SAID

Hark ye O man, and list to my Voice.
Open thy mind-space and drink of my wisdom.
Dark is the pathway of LIFE that ye travel.
Many the pitfalls that lie in thy way.

Seek ye ever to gain greater wisdom.
Attain and it shall be light on thy way.

Open thy SOUL, O man, to the Cosmic
and let it flow in as one with thy SOUL.
LIGHT is eternal, and darkness is fleeting.
Seek ye ever, O man, for the LIGHT.
Know ye that ever as Light fills thy being,
darkness for thee shall soon disappear.

Open thy souls to the BROTHERS OF BRIGHTNESS.
Let them enter and fill thee with LIGHT.
Lift up thine eyes to the LIGHT of the Cosmos.
Keep thou ever thy face to the goal.
Only by gaining the light of all wisdom,
art thou one with the Infinite goal.

Seek ye ever the Oneness eternal.
Seek ever the Light into One.
Hear ye, O man, list to my Voice
singing the song of Light and of Life.
throughout all space, Light is prevalent,
encompassing ALL with its banners it flames.
Seek ye forever in the veil of the darkness,
somewhere ye shall surely find Light.

Hidden and buried, lost to man's knowledge,
deep in the finite the Infinite exists.
Lost, but existing,
flowing through all things,
living in ALL is the INFINITE BRAIN.

In all space, there is only ONE wisdom.
Through seeming decided, it is ONE in the ONE.
All that exists comes forth from the LIGHT,
and the LIGHT comes forth from the ALL.

Everything created is based upon ORDER:
LAW rules the space where the INFINITE dwells.

Forth from equilibrium came the great cycles,
moving in harmony toward Infinity's end.
Know ye, O man, that far in the space-time,
INFINITY itself shall pass into change.
Hear ye and list to the Voice of Wisdom:

Know that ALL is of ALL evermore.
Know that through time thou may pursue wisdom
and find ever more light on the way.
Know that through time thou may pursue wisdom
and find ever more light on the way.
Aye, thou shall find that ever receding,
thy goal shall elude thee from day unto day.

Long time ago, in the HALLS OF AMENTI,
I, Thoth, stood before the LORDS of the cycles.
Mighty, THEY in their aspects of power;
mighty, THEY in the wisdom unveiled.
Led by the Dweller, first did I see them.
But afterwards free was I of their presence,
free to enter their conclave at will.
Oft did I journey down the dark pathway
unto the HALL where the LIGHT ever glows.

Learned I of the Masters of cycles,
wisdom brought from the cycles above.
Manifest THEY in this cycle
as guides of man to the knowledge of ALL.

Seven are they, mighty in power,
speaking these words through me to men.
Time after time, stood I before them
listening to words that came not with sound.

Once said THEY unto me:
O man, wouldst thou gain wisdom?
Seek for it in the heart of the flame.
Wouldst thou gain knowledge of power?

Seek ye it in the heart of the flame.
Wouldst be one with the heart of the flame?
Seek then within thine own hidden flame.

Many the times spoke THEY to me,
teaching me wisdom not of the world;
showing me ever new paths to brightness;
teaching me wisdom brought from above.
Giving knowledge of operation,
learning of LAW, the order of ALL.

Spoke to me again, the Seven, saying:
From far beyond time are WE, come, O man,
Traveled WE from beyond SPACE-TIME,
aye, from the place of Infinity's end.

And again, unto me spoke the Seven, saying:
Child of the LIGHT, O THOTH, art thou,
free to travel the bright path upward
until at last ALL ONES become ONE.

Once again, we see Thoth alluding to the fact that separation is an illusion. The truth becomes more apparent as we delve into the content of the Emerald Tablets. Consciousness has come to this realm and manifested itself as trillions of entities. The main goal is to experience itself subjectively from all aspects and perspectives of life. We are all part of the ONE. It is the WHOLE that makes up the Universal Consciousness.

AND THOTH SAID
Forth were WE formed after our order:
THREE, FOUR, FIVE, SIX, SEVEN, EIGHT--NINE.
Know ye that these are the numbers of cycles

that WE descend from unto man.
Each having here a duty to fulfill;
each having here a force to control.

Yet are we ONE with the SOUL of our cycle.
Yet are WE, too, seeking a goal.
Far beyond man's conception,
Infinity extends into a greater than ALL.

There, in a time that is yet not a time,
we shall ALL become ONE
with a greater than ALL.

Time and space are moving in circles.
Know ye their law, and ye too, shall be free.
Aye, free shall ye be to move through the cycles--
pass the guardians that dwell at the door.

Then to me spoke HE of NINE saying:
Aeons and aeons have I existed,
knowing not LIFE and tasting not death.
For know ye. O man, that far in the future,
life and death shall be one with the ALL.

Each so perfected by balancing the other
that neither exists in the Oneness of ALL.
In men of this cycle, the life force is rampant,
but life in its growth becomes one with them ALL.

Thoth is talking about becoming an ascended master and experiencing life from a higher dimension. Time is a construct of the Third dimension and is only an illusion. Time does not exist... Clocks exist. In Albert Einstein's theories of relativity, there are two types of time dilation. In special relativity, clocks that are moving with respect to (according to) a stationary observer's clock run slower. For example, if Person A moves faster than Person B, Person A will experience time at a slower rate, and a clock he is carrying will tick slower than the clock person B is carrying. The arrow of Time is an illusion. If you lived in the Fourth dimension, you would be able to see that past, future and present all at once. https://www.newscientist.com/round-up/instant-expert-general-relativity/

AND THOTH SAID
I manifest in this your cycle,
but yet am I there in your future of time.
Yet to me, time exists not,
for in my world time exists not,
for formless are WE.
Life have WE not but yet have existence,
fuller and greater and freer than thee.

Man is a flame bound to a mountain,
but WE in our cycle shall ever be free.

Know ye, O man, that when ye have progressed
into the cycle that lengthen above,
life itself will pass to the darkness
and only the essence of Soul shall remain.
Then to me spoke the LORD of the EIGHT saying:
All that ye know is but part of little.
Not as yet have ye touched on the Great.

Far out in space where LIGHT beings supreme,

came I into the LIGHT.
Formed was I also but not as ye are.

Body of Light was my formless form formed.
Know I not LIFE and know I not DEATH,
yet master am I of all that exists.

Seek ye to find the path through the barriers.
Travel the road that leads to the LIGHT.
Spoke again to me the NINE saying:
Seek ye to find the path to beyond.

Not impossible is it to grow
to a consciousness above."

For when TWO have become ONE
and ONE has become the ALL,
know ye the barrier has lifted,
and ye are made free of the road.
Grow thou from form to the formless.
Free may thou be of the road.
Thus, through ages I listened,
learning the way to the ALL.
Now Lift I my thoughts to the ALL-THING.
List ye and hear when it calls.
O LIGHT, all prevading,

One with ALL and ALL with ONE,
flow thou to me through the channel.
Enter thou so that I may be free.
Make me One with the ALL-SOUL,
shining from the blackness of night.

Free let me be of all space-time,
free from the Veil of the night.
I, a child of LIGHT, command:

Free from the darkness to be.
Formless am I to the Light-Soul,
formless yet shining with light.
Know I the bonds of the darkness
must shatter and fall before light.

Now give I this wisdom.
Free may ye be, O man,
living in light and in brightness.
Turn not they face from the Light.
Thy soul dwells in realms of brightness.
Ye are a child of the Light.

Turn thy thoughts inward not outward.
Find thou the Light-Soul within.
Know that thou art the MASTER.
All else is brought from within.
Grow thou to realms of brightness.
Hold thou thy thought on the Light.
Know thou art one with the Cosmos,
a flame and a Child of the Light.

Now to thee gave I warning:
Let not the thought turn away.
Know that the brightness
flows through thy body for aye.
Turn not to the DARK-BROTHERS
that come from the BROTHERS OF BLACK.

But keep thine eyes ever lifted,
thy soul in tune with the Light.
Take ye this wisdom and heed it.
List to my Voice and obey.
Follow the pathway to brightness,
and thou shall be ONE with the way.

Left alone, humanity is bound by its natural form and understanding, but Thoth is the supreme and ultimate Light from which emanates ultimate existence, through which he and even man, may find true consciousness.Chapter Ten

The Key of Mysteries

Emerald Tablet Eight

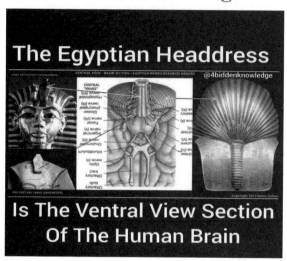

Image Credit 4biddenknowledge

Did you know that the Egyptian Headdresses worn by the Pharos have design elements that pay tribute to structures in the human brain? In the diagram above, you can see a picture of the bottom portion of the brain compared to the headdresses. That's 4biddenknowledge.

To learn more about the structures of the brain, see this article on my website: https://onsizzle.com/i/the-egyptian-headdress-4biddenknowledge-ventralview-bran-section-egyptian-nemes-headress-origins-16898845

AND THOTH SAID
Speak thou in words without voice
to those who dwell down below.
Enter the blue-litten temple
and bathe in the fire of all life.
Know, O man, thou art complex,

a being of earth and of fire.

Let thy flame shine out brightly.
Be thou only the fire.
Wisdom is hidden in darkness.
When lit by the flame of the Soul,
find thou the wisdom and be LIGHT-BORN,
a Sun of the Light without form.

Seek thee ever more wisdom.
Find it in the heart of the flame.
Know that only by striving
and Light pour into thy brain.
Now have I spoken with wisdom.
List to my Voice and obey.
Tear open the Veils of the darkness.
Shine a LIGHT on the WAY.

Speak I of Ancient Atlantis,
speak of the days
of the Kingdom of Shadows,
speak of the coming
of the children of shadows.

Out of the great deep were they called
by the wisdom of earth-men,
called for the purpose of gaining great power.

Far in the past before Atlantis existed,
men there were who delved into darkness,
using dark magic, calling up beings
from the great deep below us.

Forth came they into this cycle.
Formless were they of another vibration,
existing unseen by the children of earth-men.

Only through blood could they have formed being.
Only through man could they live in the world.
In ages past were they conquered by Masters,
driven below to the place whence they came.

But some there were who remained,
hidden in spaces and planes unknown to man.
Lived they in Atlantis as shadows,
but at times they appeared among men.
Aye, when the blood was offered,
for they came they to dwell among men.

In the form of man they amongst us,
but only to sight were they as are men.
Serpent-headed when the glamour was lifted
but appearing to man as men among men.
Crept they into the Councils,
taking forms that were like unto men.

Slaying by their arts
the chiefs of the kingdoms,
taking their form and ruling o'er man.
Only by magic could they be discovered.
Only by sound could their faces be seen.
Sought they from the Kingdom of shadows
to destroy man and rule in his place.

But, know ye, the Masters were mighty in magic,
able to lift the Veil from the face of the serpent,
able to send him back to his place.
Came they to man and taught him the secret,
the WORD that only a man can pronounce.
Swift then they lifted the Veil from the serpent
and cast him forth from the place among men.

Yet, beware, the serpent still liveth

in a place that is open at times to the world.
Unseen they walk among thee
in places where the rites have been said.
Again as time passes onward
shall they take the semblance of men."

Called may they be by the master
who knows the white or the black,
but only the white master may control
and bind them while in the flesh.

Seek not the kingdom of shadows,
for evil will surely appear.
For only the master of brightness
shall conquer the shadow of fear.
Know ye, O my brother,
that fear is an obstacle great.

Be master of all in the brightness,
the shadow will soon disappear.
Hear ye and heed my wisdom,
the voice of LIGHT is clear.
Seek not the valley of shadow,
and LIGHT will only appear.

List ye, O man,
to the depth of my wisdom.
Speak I of knowledge hidden from man.
Far have I been
on my journey through SPACE-TIME,
even to the end of space of this cycle.

Aye, glimpsed the HOUNDS of the Barrier,
lying in wait for he who would pass them.
In that space where time exists not,
faintly I sensed the guardians of cycles.

Move they only through angles.
Free are they not of the curved dimensions.

Strange and terrible
are the HOUNDS of the Barrier.
Follow they consciousness to the limits of space.
Think not to escape by entering your body,
for follow they fast the Soul through angles.
Only the circle will give ye protection,
save from the claws
of the DWELLERS IN ANGLES.

Once, in a time past,
I approached the great Barrier,
and saw on the shores where time exists not,
the formless forms
of the HOUNDS of the barrier.

Aye, hiding in the midst beyond time I found them;
and THEY, scenting me afar off,
raised themselves and gave the great bell cry
that could be heard from cycle to cycle
and moved through space toward my soul.
Fled I then fast before them,
back from time's unthinkable end.
But ever after me pursued they,
moving in strange angles not known to man.

Aye, on the gray shores of TIME-SPACE'S end
found I the HOUNDS of the Barrier,
ravening for the Soul
who attempts the beyond.
Fled I through circles back to my body.
Fled, and fast after me they followed.

Aye, after me the devourers followed,

seeking through angles to devour my Soul.

Aye, know ye man,
that the Soul who dares the Barrier
may be held in bondage
by the HOUNDS from beyond time,
held till this cycle is completed
and left behind
when the consciousness leaves.

Entered I my body.
Created the circles that know not angles,
created the form
that from my form was formed.
Made my body into a circle
and lost the pursuers in the circles of time.

But, even yet, when free from my body,
cautious ever must I be
not to move through angles,
else my soul may never be free.
Know ye, the HOUNDS of the Barrier
move only through angles
and never through curves of space.
Only by moving through curves
can ye escape them,
for in angles they will pursue thee.
O man, heed ye my warning;
Seek not to break open
the gate to beyond.

Few there are
who have succeeded in passing the Barrier
to the greater LIGHT that shines beyond.
For know ye, ever the dwellers,
seek such Souls to hold in their thrall.

Listen, O man, and heed ye my warning;
seek ye to move not in angles but curves,
And if while free from thy body,
though hearest the sound like the bay of a hound
ringing clear and bell-like through thy being,
flee back to thy body through circles,
penetrate not the midst mist before.

When thou hath entered the form thou hast dwelt in,
use thou the cross and the circle combined.
Open thy mouth and use thou thy Voice.
Utter the WORD and thou shalt be free.
Only the one who of LIGHT has the fullest
can hope to pass by the guards of the way.

And then must he move
through strange curves and angles
that are formed in direction not know to man.

List ye, O man, and heed ye my warning:
attempt not to pass the guards on the way.
Rather should ye seek to gain of thine own Light
and make thyself ready to pass on the way.
LIGHT is thine ultimate end, O my brother.
Seek and find ever the Light on the way.

CHAPTER ELEVEN

THE KEY OF FREEDOM OF SPACE

Emerald Tablet Nine

In this tablet, Thoth is telling mankind that he is a species with amnesia that is due to the cyclical rise and fall of civilizations. Humankind is constantly rising towards the light, yet to fall and be bound by darkness once again. The message in these tablets to humanity could be Thoth's way of trying to help mankind break this grueling cycle.

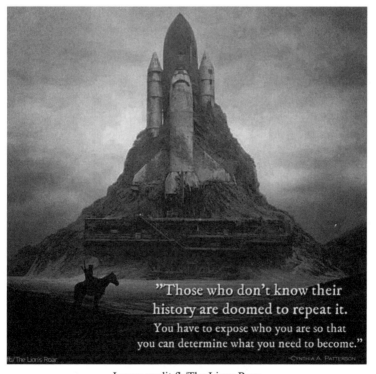

Image credit fb/The Lions Roar

AND THOTH SAID

List ye, O man, hear ye my voice,
teaching of Wisdom and Light in this cycle;
teaching ye how to banish the darkness,
teaching ye how to bring Light in thy life.

Seek ye, O man, to find the great pathway
that leads to eternal LIFE as a SUN.
Draw ye away from the veil of the darkness.
Seek to become a Light in the world.
Make of thyself a vessel for Light,
a focus for the Sun of this space.

Lift thou thine eyes to the Cosmos.
Lift thou thine eyes to the Light.
Speak in the words of the Dweller,
the chant that calls down the Light.
Sing thou the song of freedom.
Sing thou the song of the Soul.
Create the high vibration
that will make thee One with the Whole.
Blend all thyself with the Cosmos.
Grow into ONE with the Light.

Be thou a channel of order,
a pathway of LAW to the world.

Thy LIGHT, O man, is the great LIGHT,
shining through the shadow of flesh.
Free must thou rise from the darkness
before thou art One with the LIGHT.

Shadows of darkness surround thee.
Life fills thee with its flow.
But know, O man, thou must arise

and forth thy body go
far to the planes that surround thee
and yet are One with thee, too.

Look all around thee, O man.
See thine own light reflected.
Aye, even in the darkness around thee,
thine own Light pours forth through the veil.
Seek thou for wisdom always.
Let not thine body betray.
Keep in the path of the Light wave.
Shun thou the darkened way.

Know thee that wisdom is lasting.
Existing since the ALL-SOUL began,
creating harmony from by the
Law that exists in the WAY.
List ye, o man, to the teachings of wisdom.
List to the voice that speaks of the past-time.

Aye, I shall tell thee knowledge forgotten,
tell ye of wisdom hidden in past-time,
lost in the midst of darkness around me.
Know ye, man,
ye are the ultimate of all things.

Only the knowledge of this is forgotten,
lost when man was cast into bondage,
bound and fettered
by the chains of the darkness.

Long, long ago, I cast off my body.
Wandered I free
through the vastness of ether,
circled the angles
that hold man in bondage.

Know ye, O man, ye are only a spirit.
The body is nothing.
The Soul is ALL.
Let not your body be a fetter.
Cast off the darkness and travel in Light.

Cast off your body, O man, and be free,
truly a Light that is ONE with the Light.
When ye are free from the fetters of darkness
and travel in space as the SUN of the LIGHT,
then ye shall know that space in not boundless
but truly bounded by angles and curves.

Know ye, O man, that all that exists
is only an aspect of greater things yet to come.
Matter is fluid and flows like a stream,
constantly changing from one thing to another.

All through the ages has knowledge existed;
never been changed, though buried in darkness;
never been lost, though forgotten by man.

Know ye that throughout the space
that ye dwell in
are others as great as your own,
interlaced through the heart of your matter
yet separate in space of their own.

Once in a time long forgotten,
I THOTH, opened the doorway,
penetrated into other spaces
and learned of the secrets concealed.
Deep in the essence of matter
are many mysteries concealed.

Nine are the interlocked dimensions,
and Nine are the cycles of space.
Nine are the diffusions of consciousness,
and Nine are the worlds within worlds.
Aye, Nine are the Lords of the cycles
that come from above and below.

Space is filled with concealed ones,
for space is divided by time.
Seek ye the key to the time-space,
and ye shall unlock the gate.
Know ye that throughout the time-space
consciousness surely exist.
Though from our knowledge it is hidden,
yet still forever exists.

In these passages Thoth is teaching us that space is curved and partitioned and that time and space are bound together. Understanding the complexities of the curvature of space and space-time constructs, as well as spaces in two and three dimensions is a monumental undertaking. Yet, it is surely worth the effort for a greater understanding of how modern science can be used to complement the study of the Emerald Tablets and Thoth's emphasis on the space-born, time, and higher consciousness. Newton's laws of universal gravitation and of motion are explained along with Einstein's special theory of relativity, which states that measurements of space and measurements of time are interrelated. It is impossible for something to happen to the space without the time being involved in the same thing. He also discusses the intricacies of curved space in two and three dimensions.

A lengthy, famous, but highly enjoyable explanation of these ideas can be found in the lectures of one of the greatest physicist of the twentieth century, Richard Feynman. They were later presented in book format as, *The Feynman Lectures on Physics Vol. II*.

You may read the lectures by following this hyperlink:

http://www.feynmanlectures.caltech.edu/

Here is another link that contains a thrilling explanation of these ideas:
http://www.feynmanlectures.caltech.edu/II_42.html

AND THOTH SAID
The key to worlds within thee
are found only within.
For man is the gateway of mystery
and the key that is One with the One.
Seek ye within the circle.

Use the WORD I shall give.
Open the gateway within thee,
and surely thou, too, shall live.
Man, ye think that ye liveth,
but know it is life within death.
For as sure as ye are bound to your body,
for you no life exists.
Only the Soul is space-free,
has life that is really a life.

All else is only a bondage,
a fetter from which to be free.
Think not that man is earth-born,
though come from the earth he may be.

Man is light-born spirit.
But, without knowing, he can never be free.
Darkness surrounds the light-born.
Darkness fetters the Soul.

Only the one who is seeking
may ever hope to be free.
Shadows around thee are falling
darkness fills all the space

Shine forth, O LIGHT of the man-soul.
Fill thou the darkness of space.
Ye are son of the GREAT LIGHT

Remember and ye shall be free.

Stay not thou in the shadows.
Spring forth from the darkness of night
Light, let thy Soul be, O SUN-BORN,
fill with glory of Light,
Freed from the bonds of the darkness,
a Soul that is One with the Light.

Thou art the key to all wisdom.
Within thee is all time and space.
Live not in bondage to darkness.
Free thou, thy Light-form from night.

Great Light that fills all the Cosmos,
flow thou fully to man.
Make of his body a light-torch
that shall never be quenched among men.

Long in the past, sought I wisdom,
knowledge not known to man.
Far to the past, I traveled
into the space where time began.
Sought I ever knew knowledge
to add to the wisdom I knew.
Yet only, I found, did the future
hold the key to the wisdom I thought.

Down, to the HOLES of AMENTI
I journeyed, the greater knowledge to seek.
Ask of thee, LORDS of the CYCLES,
they way to the wisdom I sought.

Asked the LORDS this question:
Where is the source of ALL?
Answered, in tones that were mighty,

the voice of the LORD of the NINE:
Free thou thy soul from thy body
and come forth with me to the LIGHT.

Forth I came from my body,
a glittering flame in the night.
Stood I before the LORD,
bathed in the fire of LIFE.
Seized was I then by a force,
great beyond knowledge of man.

Cast was I to the Abyss
through spaces unknown to man.
Saw I the moldings of Order
from the chaos and angles of night.
Saw I the LIGHT, spring from Order
and heard the voice of the Light.
Saw I the flame of the Abyss,
casting forth Order and Light.
Saw Order spring out of chaos.
Saw Light giving forth Life.

Then heard I the voice.
Hear thou and understand.
The flame is the source of all things,
containing all things in potentiality.

The Order that sent forth light
is the WORD and from the WORD,
COME LIFE and the existence of all.
And again spoke the voice saying:
THE LIFE in thee is the WORD.
Find thou the LIFE within thee
and have powers to use of the WORD.

Long I watched the Light-flame,

pouring forth from the Essence of Fire,
realizing that LIFE but Order
and that man is one with the fire.
Back I came to my body
stood again with the Nine,
listened to the voice of the Cycles,
vibrate with powers they spoke:

Know ye, O Thoth, that LIFE
is but thee WORD of the FIRE.
The LIFE forth ye seek before thee
is but the WORD in the World as a fire.
Seek ye the path to the WORD and Powers
shall surely be thine.

Then asked I of the Nine:
O Lord, show me the path.
Give the path to the wisdom.
Show me the way to the WORD.
Answered, me then,
the LORD OF THE NINE:
Through ORDER, ye shall find the way.
Saw ye that the WORD came from Chaos?
Saw ye not that LIGHT came from FIRE?

Look in thy life for this order.
Balance and order thy life.
Quell all the Chaos of the emotions
and thou shalt have order in LIFE.
ORDER brought forth from Chaos
will bring thee the WORD of the SOURCE,
will thee the power of CYCLES,
and make of thy Soul a force that
free will extend through the ages,
a perfect SUN from the Source.

Listened I to the voice
and deep thanked the words in my heart.
Forever have I sought for order
that I might draw on the WORD.

Know ye that he who attains it
must ever in ORDER be for use
of the WORD though this order
has never and can never be.
Take ye these words, O man.
As part of thy life, let them be.
Seek thee to conquer this order
and One with the WORD thou shalt be.

Put forth thy effort in gaining LIGHT
on the pathway of Life.
Seek to be One with the SUN/state.
Seek to be solely the LIGHT.
Hold thou thy thought on the Oneness
of Light with the body of man.
Know that all is Order from Chaos
born into light.

CHAPTER TWELVE

THE KEY OF TIME

Emerald Tablet Ten

AND THOTH SAID

List ye, O Man, Take of my wisdom.
Learn of his deep hidden mysteries of space.
Learn of the THOUGHT that grew in the abyss,
bringing Order and Harmony in space.

Know ye, O man, that all exists
has being only because of the LAW.
Know ye the LAW and ye shall be free,
never be bound by the fetters of night.

Far, through strange spaces, have I journeyed
into the depth of the abyss of time,
until in the end all was revealed.

Know ye that mystery is only mystery
when it is knowledge unknown to man.
When ye have plumbed the heart of all mystery,
knowledge and wisdom will surely be thine.

Seek ye and learn that TIME is the secret
whereby ye may be free of this space.

Image Courtesy of 4biddenknowledge

Thoth is telling us AGAIN what the sages of old have been saying for eons. Time does not exist... Clocks exist. When your scientists figure this out they will rediscover what the ancients knew. According to Albert Einstein's theories of relativity, two types of time dilation exist. The theory of special relativity explains how there is a difference of time that elapses between two events as measured by observers. For example, if one person moves faster than another person, then the first person will experience time at a slower rate, and the clock the faster person is carrying will tick slower than the clock the second person is carrying. With this understanding, it's not so difficult to accept the fact that the arrow of Time is an illusion. If you lived in the 4th dimension or higher, you would be able to see past, present, and future all at once. In general relativity, clocks that are near to the strong gravitational field of a planet, run slower.

AND THOTH SAID

Long have I, [the god of] Wisdom, sought wisdom;
aye, and shall seek of eternity's end
for know that ever before me receding
shall move the goal I seek to attain.

Even the Lords of the Cycles
know that not yet have they reached the goal,
For with all of their wisdom,
they know that Truth ever grows.

Once, in a past time, I spoke to the Dweller.
Asked of the mystery of time and space.
Asked him the question that surged in my being,
saying: O Master, what is time?

Then to me spoke HE, the Master:
Know ye, O Thoth, in the beginning
there was VOID and nothingness,
a timeless, spaceless, nothingness.

And into the nothingness came a thought,
purposeful, all-pervading,
and It filled the Void.

There existed no matter, only force,
a movement, a vortex, or vibration
of the purposeful thought
that filled the Void.

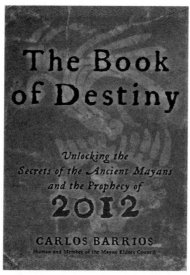

https://www.harpercollins.com/9780061833830/the-book-of-destiny/

Nobel Laureate Ernesto Sabato wrote that "Face to face with the schism caused by rational and scientific thought, Carlos Barrios undertakes an authentic and passionate search, bringing us close to the Cosmovision of one of the most ancient and wise people of our continent."

According to HarperCollins Press, "James Redfield's *The Celestine Prophecy* and the writings of Nostradamus meet Don Miguel Ruiz's

The Four Agreements and Carolyn Myss' *Anatomy of the Spirit, Sacred Contracts* in *The Book of Destiny: Unlocking the Secrets of the Ancient Mayans and the Prophecy of 2012.* A contemporary Mayan Priest and Shaman reveals the genius of the ancient Mayan calendar and its accompanying horoscope, and examines in depth the ancient 2012 prophecy. *The Book of Destiny* is the most complete and authentic book on the secrets of the ancient Mayan culture and what it means for readers today." It is a companion read to the Emerald Tablets of Thoth as it allows us to go into the world of the Ancient Mayan civilization, understanding them better as an Atlantean colony.

AND THOTH SAID

And I questioned the Master, saying:
Was this thought eternal?
And answered me the Dweller, saying:
In the beginning, there was eternal thought,
and for thought to be eternal, time must exist.

So into the all-pervading thought
grew the LAW of TIME.
Aye time which exists through all space,
floating in a smooth, rhythmic movement
that is eternally in a state of fixation.

Time changes not,
but all things change in time.
For time is the force
that holds events separate,
each in its own proper place.
Time is not in motion,
but ye move through time
as your consciousness
moves from one event to another.

Aye, by time yet exist, all in all,
an eternal ONE existence.
Know ye that even though in the time ye are separate,
yet still are ONE, in all times existent.

George Gurdjieff claimed, "Man lives his life in sleep, and in sleep he dies." In other words, he was saying that people cannot perceive reality in their current states because they do not possess a unified consciousness, but rather, live in a state of a hypnotic, waking sleep. Gurdjieff's claim was that humans live in a waking dream and only dream that they are awake. This state of "waking sleep" is also called "relative consciousness." It is the level of consciousness that ordinary humans are born into, live their lives, and then die in, never waking to into the more objective states of awareness. Because most humans are walking around in a state of waking sleep, they are never able to know who they truly are, and therefore, they remain unaware of their true motivations and the causal forces which motivate them in their daily choices and activities. In conclusion, when humans cannot determine their true motivations and remain unaware, they lie to themselves, and thus, their entire lives are lies.

Reference: *In Search of the Miraculous,* by P.D. Ouspensky.

AND THOTH SAID
Ceased then the voice of the DWELLER,
and departed I to ponder on time.
For knew I that in these words lay wisdom
and a way to explore the mysteries of time.
Oft did I ponder the words of the DWELLER.
Then sought I to solve the mystery of time.
Found I that time moves through strange angles.
Yet only by curves could I hope to attain the key
that would give me access to the time-space.
Found I that only by moving upward
and yet again by moving to right-ward
could I be free from the time of the movement.

Forth I came from out of my body,
moved in the movements that changed me in time.
Strange were the sights I saw in my journeys,
many the mysteries that opened to view.
Aye, saw I man's beginning,
learned from the past that nothing is new.

Seek ye, O man, to learn the pathway
that leads through the spaces
that are formed forth in time.

Forget not, O man, with all of thy seeking
that Light is the goal ye shall seek to attain.
Search ye for the Light on thy pathway
and ever for thee the goal shall endure.
Let not thine heart turn ever to darkness.
light let shine Soul be, a Sun on the way.
Know ye that eternal brightness,
ya shall ever find thy Soul hid in Light,
never fettered by bondage or darkness,
ever it shines forth a Sun of the Light.

Aye, know, though hidden in darkness,
your Soul, a spark of the true flame, exists.
Be ye One with the greatest of all Lights.
Find at the SOURCE, the END of thy goal.
Light is life, for without the great Light
nothing can ever exist.

Know ye, that in all formed matter,
the heart of Light always exists.
Aye, even though bound in the darkness,
inherent Light always exists.
Once I stood in the HALLS OF AMENTI
and heard the voice of the LORDS of AMENTI,
saying in tones that rang through the silence,
words of power, mighty and potent.
Chanted they the song of the cycles,
the words that open the path to beyond.

Aye, I saw the great path opened
and looked for the instant into the beyond.
Saw I the movements of the cycles,

vast as the thought of the SOURCE could convey.
Knew I then even Infinity
is moving on to some unthinkable end.

Saw I that the Cosmos is Order
and part of a movement that extends to all space,
a party of an Order of Orders,
constantly moving in a harmony of space.

Saw I the wheeling of cycles
like vast circles across the sky.
Knew I then that all that has being
is growing to meet yet another being
in a far-off grouping of space and of time.
Knew I then that in Words are power
to open the planes that are hidden from man.
Aye, that even in Words lies hidden the key
that will open above and below.

Hark ye, now man, this word I leave with thee.
Use it and ye shall find power in its sound.
Say ye the word:
"ZIN-URU"
and power ye shall find.

Yet must ye understand that man is of Light
and Light is of man.

List ye, O man, and hear a mystery
stranger than all that lies 'neath the Sun.
Know ye, O man, that all space
is filled by worlds within worlds;
aye, one within the other yet separate by Law.

Once in my search for deep buried wisdom,
I opened the door that bars THEM from man.

Called I from the other planes of being,
one who was fairer than the daughters of men.

Aye, I called her from out of the spaces,
to shine as a Light in the world of men.
Used I the drum of the Serpent.
Wore I the robe of the purple and gold.
Placed on my head, I, the crown of Silver.
Around me the circle of cinnabar shone.
Raised I my arms and cried the invocation
that opens the path to the planes beyond,
cried to the LORDS of the SIGNS in their houses:
Lords of the two horizons,
watchers of the treble gates,
stand ye One at the right and One at the left
as the STAR rises to his throne
and rules over his sign.

Aye, thou dark prince of ARULU,
open the gates of the dim, hidden land
and release her whom ye keep imprisoned.
Hear ye, hear ye, hear ye,
dark Lords and Shining Ones,
and by their secret names,
names which I know and can pronounce,
hear ye and obey my will.

Lit I then with flame my circle
and called HER in the space-planes beyond.
Daughter of Light return from ARULU.
Seven times and seven times
have I passed through the fire.
Food have I not eaten.
Water have I not drunk.
I call thee from ARULU,
from the realms of EKERSHEGAL.

I summon thee, lady of Light.

Then before me rose the dark figures;
aye, the figures of the Lords of Arulu.
Parted they before me
and forth came the Lady of Light.
Free was she now from the LORDS of the night,
free to live in the Light of the earth Sun,
free to live as a child of the Light.
Hear ye and listen, O my children.

Magic is knowledge and only is Law.
Be not afraid of the power within thee
for it follows Law as the stars in the sky.
Know ye that to be without knowledge,
wisdom is magic and not of the Law.
But know ye that ever ye by your knowledge
can approach closer to a place in the Sun.

List ye, my children, follow my teaching.
Be ye ever seeker of Light.
Shine in the world of men all around thee,
a Light on the path that shall shine among men.

Follow ye and learn of my magic.
Know that all force is thine if thou wilt.
Fear not the path that leads thee to knowledge,
but rather shun ye the dark road.

Light is thine, O man, for the taking.
Cast off the fetters and thou shalt be free.
Know ye that they Soul is living in bondage
fettered by fears that hold ye in thrall.

Open thy eyes and see the great sunlight.
Be not afraid for all is thine own.

Fear is the LORD of the dark ARULU
to he who never faced the dark fear.
Aye, know that fear has existence
created by those who are bound by their fears.
Shake off thy bondage, O children,
and walk in the Light of the glorious day.

Never turn they thoughts to the darkness
and surely ye shall be One with the Light.
Man is only what he believeth,
a brother of darkness or a child of the Light.
Come though into the Light my Children.

Walk in the pathway that leads to the Sun.
Hark ye now, and list to the wisdom.
Use thou the word I have given unto thee.
Use it and surely though shalt find power and wisdom
and Light to walk in the way.
Seek thee and find the key I have given
and ever shalt thou be a Child of the Light.

CHAPTER THIRTEEN

The Key to Above and Below

Emerald Tablet Eleven

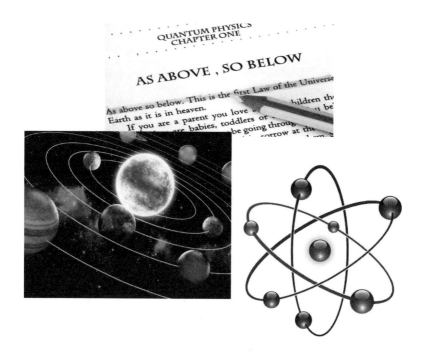

AND THOTH SAID

Hear ye and list ye, O children of Khem,
to the words that I give that shall bring ye to the Light.
Ye know, O men, that I knew your fathers,
aye, your fathers in a time long ago.
Deathless have I been through all the ages,
living among ye since your knowledge began.

Leading ye upward to the Light of the Great Soul

have I ever striven,
drawing ye from out of the darkness of night.

Know ye, O people amongst whom I walk,
that I, *Thoth*, have all of the knowledge
and all of the wisdom known, to man since the ancient days
Keeper have I been of the secrets of the great race,
holder of the key that leads into life.

Bringer up have I been to ye, O my children,
even from the darkness of the *Ancient of Days*.
List ye now to the words of my wisdom.
List ye now to the message I bring.
Hear ye now the words I give thee, and
ye shall be raised from the darkness to *Light*.

Far in the past, when first I came to thee,
found I thee in caves of rocks.

Lifted I thee by my power and wisdom
until thou didst shine as men among men.
Aye, found I thee without any knowing.
Only a little were ye raised beyond beasts.
Fanned I ever the spark of thy consciousness
until at last ye flamed as men.

Thoth is letting the humans know that he has something really important to say and that they should listen because is wisdom and knowledge ancient and surpassing.

AND THOTH SAID
Now shall I speak to thee knowledge ancient
beyond the thought of thy race.
Know ye that we of the *Great Race*
had and have knowledge that is more than man's.
Wisdom we gained from the star-born races,
wisdom and knowledge far beyond man.

Down to us had descended the masters of wisdom
as far beyond us as I am from thee.
List ye now while I give ye wisdom.
Use it and free thou shalt be.

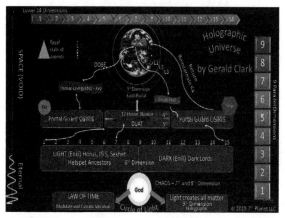

Image Credit Gerald Clark - Author – 7th Planet Mercury
Rising – Holographic Simulator

AND THOTH SAID

Know ye that in the pyramid I builded are the Keys
that shall show ye the Way into life.
Aye, draw ye a line from the great image I builded,
to the apex of the pyramid, built as a gateway.
Draw ye another opposite in the same angle and direction.
Dig ye and find that which I have hidden.
There shall ye find the underground entrance to
the secrets hidden before ye were men.

As I stated earlier in the book, these underground passages and
rooms have already been discovered.

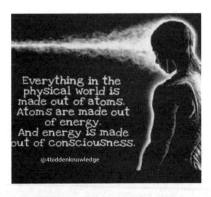

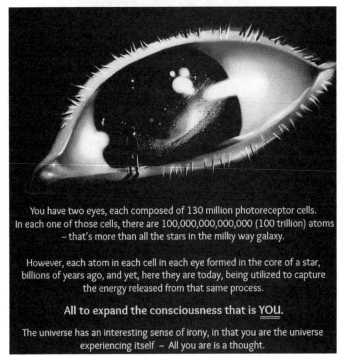

You have two eyes, each composed of 130 million photoreceptor cells.
In each one of those cells, there are 100,000,000,000,000 (100 trillion) atoms
– that's more than all the stars in the milky way galaxy.

However, each atom in each cell in each eye formed in the core of a star,
billions of years ago, and yet, here they are today, being utilized to capture
the energy released from that same process.

All to expand the consciousness that is YOU.

The universe has an interesting sense of irony, in that you are the universe
experiencing itself – All you are is a thought.

AND THOTH SAID

Tell ye I now of the mystery of cycles
that move in movements that are strange to the finite,
for infinite are they beyond knowledge of man.
Know ye that there are nine of the cycles;
aye, nine above and fourteen below,
moving in harmony to the place of joining

that shall exist in the future of time.

Know ye that the Lords of the Cycles
are units of consciousness sent from the others to unify
This with the All.

Highest are They of the consciousness
of all the Cycles, working in harmony with the Law.

Know They that in time all will be perfected,
having none above and none below, but all One
in a perfected Infinity, a harmony of all in the Oneness of All.
Deep neath the Earth surface in the Halls of Amenti
sit the Seven, the Lords of the Cycles,
aye, and another, the Lord from below.
Yet know thee that in Infinity there is
neither above nor below.
But ever there is and ever shall be
Oneness of All when all is complete.

Oft have I stood before the Lords of the All.
Oft at the fount of their wisdom have drunken and
filled both my body and Soul with their Light.
Spake they to me and told me of cycles
and the Law that gives them the means to exist.
Aye, spake to me the Lord of the Nine saying:

O, Thoth, great are ye among Earth children,
but mysteries exist of which ye know not.
Ye know that ye came from a space-time below
this and know ye shall travel to a space-time beyond.
But little ye know of the mysteries within them,
little ye know of the wisdom beyond. Know ye that
ye as a whole in this consciousness
are only a cell in the process of growth.

The consciousness below thee is ever-expanding
in different ways from those known to thee.
Aye, it, though in space-time below thee,
is ever growing in ways that are different from
those that were part of the ways of thine own.

For know that it grows as a result of thy growth
but not in the same way that thou didst grow.
The growth that thou had and have in the present
have brought into being a cause and effect.

No consciousness follows the path of those before it,
else all would be repetition and vain.
Each consciousness in the cycle it exists in
follows its own path to the ultimate goal.
Each plays its part in the Plan of the Cosmos.

Each plays its part in the ultimate end.
The farther the cycle, the greater its
knowledge and ability to blend the Law of the whole.
Know ye, that ye in the cycles below us
are working the minor parts of the Law,
while we of the cycle that extends to Infinity
take of the striving and build greater Law.

Each has his own part to play in the cycles.
Each has his work to complete in his way.
The cycle below thee is yet not below thee
but only formed for a need that exists.
For know ye that the fountain of wisdom
that sends forth the cycles is eternally
seeking new powers to gain.

Ye know that knowledge is gained only by practice,
and wisdom comes forth only from knowledge,
and thus are the cycles created by Law.

Means are they for the gaining of knowledge
for the Plane of Law that is the Source of the All.
The cycle below is not truly below but only
different in space and in time.

The consciousness there is working and
testing lesser things than those ye are.
And know, just as ye are working on greater,
so above ye are those who are also working
as ye are on yet other laws.

The difference that exists between the cycles
is only in ability to work with the Law.
We, who have being in cycles beyond thee,
are those who first came forth from the
Source and have in the passage through
time-space gained ability to use
Laws of the Greater that are far beyond
the conception of man.

Nothing there is that is really below thee
but only a different operation of Law.
Look thee above or look thee below,
the same shall ye find.
For all is but part of the Oneness
that is at the Source of the Law.

The consciousness below thee is
part thine own as we are a part of thine.
Ye, as a child had not the knowledge
that came to ye when ye became a man.

Compare ye the cycles to man in his journey
from birth unto death,
and see in the cycle below thee the child
with the knowledge he has;

and see ye yourself as the child grown older,
advancing in knowledge as time passes on.
See ye, We, also, the child grown to manhood
with the knowledge and wisdom that came
with the years.

So also, O Thoth, are the cycles of consciousness,
children in different stages of growth,
yet all from the one Source, the Wisdom,
and all to the Wisdom returning again.
Ceased then He from speaking and sat
in the silence that comes to the Lords.

Then again spake He unto me, saying:
Oh Thoth, long have We sat in Amenti,
guarding the flame of life in the Halls.
Yet know, we are still part of our
Cycles with our Vision reaching unto them and beyond.

Aye, know we that of all,
nothing else matters accepting the growth
we can gain with our Soul.
Know we the flesh is fleeting.
The things men count great are nothing to us.
The things we seek are not of the body
but are only the perfected state of the Soul.
When ye as men can learn that nothing but
progress of Soul can count in the end,
then truly ye are free from all bondage,
free to work in a harmony of Law.

Know, O man, ye should aim at perfection,
for only thus can ye attain to the goal.
Though ye should know that nothing is perfect,
yet it should be thy aim and thy goal.
Ceased again the voice of the Nine,

and into my consciousness the words had sunk.
Now, seek I ever more wisdom
that I may be perfect in Law with the All.

Soon go I down to the Halls of Amenti
to live beneath the cold flower of life.
Ye whom I have taught shall nevermore see me.
Yet live I forever in the wisdom I taught.
All that man is is because of his wisdom.
All that he shall be is the result of his cause.

List ye, now to my voice and become
greater than common man.
Lift thine eyes upward,
let Light fill thy being,
be thou ever Children of Light.
Only by effort shall ye grow upward to
the plane where Light is the All of the All.
Be ye the master of all that surrounds thee.

Never be mastered by the effects of thy life.
Create then ever more perfect causes
and in time shalt thou be a Sun of the Light
Free, let thine soul soar ever upward,
free from the bondage and fetters of night.

Lift thine eyes to the Sun in the sky-space.
For thee, let it be a symbol of life.
Know that thou art the Greater Light,
perfect in thine own sphere,
when thou art free.

Look not ever into the blackness.
Lift up thine eyes to the space above.
Free let thine Light flame upward
and shalt thou be a Child of the Light.

CHAPTER FOURTEEN

THE LAW OF CAUSE AND EFFECT AND THE KEY OF PROPHECY

Emerald Tablet Twelve

When it comes to learning about cause and effect, a word that you may encounter is *Causality*. Causality refers to the relationship between cause and effect and states that everything has a cause. Also known as causation, it connects one process (the cause) with another process or state (the effect), where the first is partly responsible for the second, and the second is partly dependent on the first. From *Dialectical Materialism* by A. Spirkin.

For a more complete understanding of causality, follow the hyperlink below:

https://www.marxists.org/reference/archive/spirkin/works/dialectical.../ch02-s06.html

AND THOTH SAID
List ye, O man, to the words of my wisdom,
list to the voice of *Thoth, the Atlantean.*
Conquered have I the *Law* of time-space.
Knowledge have I gained of the future of time.

Know I that man in his movement through
space-time shall ever be *One* with the *All*

Know ye, O man,
that all of the future is an open book
to him who can read.
All effect shall bring forth its causes
as all effects grew from the first cause.
Know ye the future is not fixed or

stable but varies as cause brings forth an effect.
Look in the cause thou shalt bring into being,
and surely thou shalt see that all is effect.

So, O man, be sure the effects that ye bring
forth are ever causes of more perfect effects.
Know ye the future is never in fixation but
follows man's free will as it moves through
the movements of time-space toward
the goal where a new time begins.
Man can only read the future through
the causes that bring the effects.
Seek ye within the causation and
surely ye shall find the effects.

List ye, O man, while I speak of the future,
speak of the effect that follows the cause.
Know ye that man in his journey light-ward
is ever seeking escape from the night that surrounds him,
like the shadows that surround the stars in the sky
and like the stars in the sky-space, he, too,
shall shine from the shadows of night.

Ever his destiny shall lead him onward
until he is One with the Light.
Aye, though his way lies midst the shadows,
ever before him glows the Great Light.
Dark though the way be yet shall he conquer
the shadows that flow around him like night.

Thoth is eluding to the fact that the Law Of Attraction can be used to forecast the future. In other words, by using the Law of Attraction we have the ability to attract whatever we focus on into our lives. Regardless of our background or who we are, everyone is governed by Universal Law, including the Law of Attraction. It is this law that harnesses the power of the mind and creates our reality. Therefore, I believe it wise to not waste a single thought on those things that are destructive, negative, or harmful. Instead, focus your thoughts on positivity, gratitude, and all the things that bring peace and delight to your heart and soul. Only then will you will find yourself living a life of joy and satisfaction.

Here is an exercise that may make it easier for you to implement into your daily life:

Imagine your thoughts as money. Do not spend them on frivolous things. Invest your thoughts wisely.

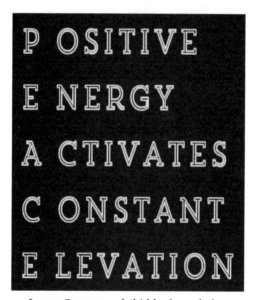

Image Courtesy of 4biddenknowledge

This is why the universe is such an infinitely beautiful place. The Law of Attraction dictates that whatever can be imagined and held in the mind's eye is achievable if you take action on a plan to get to where you want to be.

Thoth is also saying the future is not fixed, but it can still be read. Again, I believe that Thoth is trying to give us the guided steps to break the cycle of rise and fall. It seems his ultimate goal is to help mankind ascend to higher dimensions and permanently break the cycle of reincarnation into the Third dimensional holographic universe.

AND THOTH SAID

Far in the future, I see man as *Light-born*,
free from the darkness that fetters the *Soul,*

living in Light without the bounds of the darkness
to cover the Light that is Light of their Soul.

Know ye, O man, before ye attain this that
many the dark shadows shall fall on your Light
striving to quench with the shadows of darkness
the Light of the Soul that strives to be free.

Great is the struggle between Light and darkness,
age old and yet ever new. Yet, know in a time, far in the future,
Light shall be All and darkness shall fall.

List ye, O man, to my words of wisdom.
Prepare and ye shall not bind your Light.
Man has risen and man has fallen as ever new
waves of consciousness flow from the great
abyss below us toward the Sun of their goal.

Ye, my children, have risen from a state
that was little above the beast,
until now of all men ye are greatest.
Yet before thee were others greater than thee.
Yet tell I thee as before thee others have fallen,
so also shall ye come to an end.

And upon the land where ye dwell now,
barbarians shall dwell and in turn rise to Light.
Forgotten shall be the ancient-wisdom,
yet ever shall live though hidden from men.
Aye, in the land thou callest Khem,
races shall rise and races shall fall.
Forgotten shalt thou be of the children of men.

Yet thou shalt have moved to a star-space
beyond this leaving behind this place where thou has dwelt.
The Soul of man moves ever onward,

bound not by any one star.

But ever moving to the great goal before him
where he is dissolved in the Light of the All.
Know ye that ye shall ever go onward,
moved by the Law of cause and effect
until in the end both become One
Aye, man, after ye have gone,
others shall move in the places ye lived.
Knowledge and wisdom shall all be forgotten,
and only a memory of Gods shall survive.
As I to thee am a God by my knowledge,
so ye, too shall be Gods of the future
because of your knowledge far above theirs.

Yet know ye that all through the ages,
man shall have access to Law when he will.
Ages to come shall see revival of wisdom
to those who shall inherit thy place on this star.
They shall, in turn, come into wisdom
and learn to banish the darkness by Light.
Yet greatly must they strive through the ages
to bring unto themselves the freedom of Light.

Then shall there come unto man the great warfare
that shall make the Earth tremble and shake in its course.
Aye, then shall the Dark Brothers
open the warfare between Light and the night.
When man again shall conquer the ocean and fly
in the air on wings like the birds;
when he has learned to harness the lightning,
then shall the time of warfare begin.
Great shall the battle be twixt the forces,
great the warfare of darkness and Light.

Nation shall rise against nation

using the dark forces to shatter the Earth.
Weapons of force shall wipe out the Earth-man
until half of the races of men shall be gone."

Sounds very similar to a verse in the Bible. I wonder where the writers of the Bible copied this? Matthew 24:7 "For nation shall rise against nation, and kingdom against kingdom: and there shall be famines, and pestilences, and earthquakes, in divers places."

AND THOTH SAID

Then shall come forth the *Sons of the Morning*
and give their edict to the children of men, saying:
O men, cease from thy striving against thy brother.
Only thus can ye come to the Light.
Cease from thy unbelief, O my brother,
and follow the path and know ye are right.

Then shall men cease from their striving,
brother against brother and father against son.
Then shall the ancient home of my people rise
from its place beneath the dark ocean waves.

Then shall the *Age of Light* be unfolded
with all men seeking the *Light* of the goal.
Then shall the *Brothers of Light* rule the people.
Banished shall be the darkness of night

.

At first glance, this passage resonates with the biblical reference to brother against brother and father against son. But that is a common characteristic in many cultures. Such behavior, however, sparks interest from Atlantis. Thoth is referencing the Golden Age. A Golden Age can be found in all religions. It speaks of a period of primordial peace, harmony, stability, and prosperity. During that Golden Age of Atlantas, peace and harmony prevailed, people did not have to work to feed themselves; the earth provided food in abundance. The Atlanteans lived to a very old age with a youthful appearance, eventually dying peacefully, with spirits living on as 'guardians.' Plato in Cratylus (397 e) recounts the golden race of humans who came first. He clarifies that Hesiod did not mean literally made of gold, but good and noble. Atlantean's will resurface from their homes beneath the seas to initiate the Golden Age.

AND THOTH SAID

Aye, the children of men shall progress
onward and upward to the great goal.
Children of Light shall they become.
Flame of the flame shall their *Souls* ever be.
Knowledge and wisdom shall be man's
in the great age for he shall approach the eternal flame,
the *Source* of all wisdom,
the place of beginning,
that is yet *One* with the end of all things."
When that happens, according to Thoth, 'Knowledge and wisdom
shall be man's
in the great age.'

Aye, in a time that is yet unborn,
all shall be One and One shall be All.
Man, a perfect flame of this Cosmos,
shall move forward to a place in the stars.

Aye, shall move even from out of this space-time
into another beyond the stars.
Long have ye listened to me,
O my children,
long have ye listened to the wisdom of Thoth.

Now I depart from ye into darkness.
Now go I to the Halls of Amenti,
there to dwell in the future when Light
shall come again to man.
Yet, know ye, my Spirit shall ever be with thee,
guiding thy feet in the pathway of Light.
Guard ye the secrets I leave with thee,
and surely my spirit will guard thee through life.

Keep thine eyes ever on the pathway to wisdom.
Keep the Light as thy goal evermore.
Fetter not thy Soul in bondage of darkness;
free let it wing in its flight to the stars.
Now I depart thee to dwell in Amenti.
Be thou my children in this life and the next.

The time will come when ye, too, shall be deathless,
living from age to age a Light among men.
Guard ye the entrance to the Halls of Amenti.
Guard ye the secrets I have hidden among ye.
Let not the wisdom be cast to barbarians.
Secret shall thou keep it for those who seek Light.
Now depart I.

Receive thou my blessing.
Take thou my way and follow the Light.
Blend thou thy Soul in the Great Essence.
One, with the Great Light let thy consciousness be.
Call thou on me when thou dost need me.
Use my name three times in a row:
Chequetet, Arelich, Volmalites.

CHAPTER FIFTEEN

THE KEY OF LIFE AND DEATH

Emerald Tablet Thirteen

AND THOTH SAID
List ye, O man, hear ye the wisdom.
Hear ye the Word that shall fill thee with Life.
Hear ye the Word that shall banish the darkness.
Hear ye the voice that shall banish the night.
Mystery and wisdom have I brought to my children;
knowledge and power descended from old.

Know ye not that all shall be opened
when ye shall find the oneness of all?
One shall ye be with the Masters of Mystery,
Conquerors of Death and Masters of Life.

Aye, ye shall learn of the flower of Amenti
the blossom of life that shines in the Halls.
In Spirit shall ye reach that Halls of Amenti
and bring back the wisdom that liveth in Light.
Know ye the gateway to power is secret.
Know ye the gateway to life is through death.

Aye, through death but not as ye know death,
but a death that is life and is fire and is Light.
Desireth thou to know the deep, hidden secret?
Look in thy heart where the knowledge is bound.
Know that in thee the secret is hidden,
the source of all life and the source of all death.

List ye, O man, while I tell the secret,

reveal unto thee the secret of old.
Deep in Earth's heart lies the flower,
the source of the Spirit
that binds all in its form.
or know ye that the Earth is living in body
as thou art alive in thine own formed form.

The Flower of Life is as thine own place of Spirit
and streams through the Earth
as thine flows through thy form;
giving of life to the Earth and its children,
renewing the Spirit from form unto form.
This is the Spirit that is form of thy body,
shaping and molding into its form.

Know ye, O man, that thy form is dual,
balanced in polarity while formed in its form.
Know that when fast on thee *Death* approaches,
it is only because thy balance is shaken.
It is only because one pole has been lost.

Yin Yang Flower of Life

The Flower of Life is a geometric shape that is comprised of numerous, overlapping and evenly-spaced circles. The circles are arranged in a flower-like pattern with six-fold symmetry. Throughout the ages, philosophers, architects, and artists have known of the perfect form, proportions, and harmony of the Flower of Life. Only recently is quantum physics recognizing that the Flower of Life is a depiction of the source field, which simultaneously connects every particle and allows consciousness to collapse waves into matter.

AND THOTH SAID

Know that the secret of life in Amenti
is the secret of restoring the balance of poles.
All that exists has form and is living
because of the Spirit of life in its poles.

See ye not that in Earth's heart
is the balance of all things that exist
and have being on its face?
The source of thy Spirit is drawn from Earth's heart,
for in thy form thou are one with the Earth
When thou hast learned to hold thine own balance,
then shalt thou draw on the balance of Earth.

Exist then shalt thou while Earth is existing,
changing in form, only when Earth, too, shalt change:
Tasting not of death, but one with this planet,
holding thy form till all pass away.

List ye, O man, whilst I give the secret so that
ye, too, shalt taste not of change.
One hour each day shalt thou lie
with thine head pointed to the
place of the positive pole (north).
One hour each day shalt thy head be
pointed to the place of the negative pole (south).
Whilst thy head is placed to the northward,
hold thou thy consciousness from the chest to the head.

And when thy head is placed southward,
hold thou thy thought from chest to the feet.
Hold thou in balance once in each seven,
and thy balance will retain the whole of its strength.
Aye, if thou be old, thy body will freshen
and thy strength will become as a youth's.

In the passages above, Thoth is talking about aligning one's chakras within the body and harnessing the energy from the Earth's north and south poles. This is very similar to how we use batteries in today's world. To learn about how batteries work, check out the link below:

https://physics.stackexchange.com/q/391827

AND THOTH SAID
This is the secret known to the Masters
by which they hold off the fingers of Death.
Neglect not to follow the path I have shown,
for when thou hast passed beyond years
to a hundred to neglect
it will mean the coming of Death.
Hear ye, my words, and follow the pathway.
Keep thou thy balance and live on in life.

Hear ye, O man, and list to my voice.
List to the wisdom that gives thee of *Death*.
When at the end of thy work appointed,
thou may desire to pass from this life,
pass to the plane where the *Suns of the Morning*
live and have being as *Children of Light*.
Pass without pain and pass without sorrow
into the plane where is eternal *Light*.

First lie at rest with thine head to the eastward.
Fold thou thy hands at the Source of thy life [solar plexus].

Place thou thy consciousness in the life seat.
Whirl it and divide to north and to south.

Send thou the one out toward the northward.
Send thou the other out to the south.
Relax thou their hold upon thy being.
Forth from thy form will thy silver spark fly,
upward and onward to the Sun of the morning,
blending with Light, at one with its source.

There it shall flame till desire shall be created.
Then shall return to a place in a form.

Know ye, O men, that thus pass the great Souls,
changing at will from life unto life.
Thus ever passes the Avatar,
willing his Death as he wills his own life.

Thoth has made another direct reference to reincarnation and transferring one's consciousness into new avatars. This ability to transcend death and incarnate at will is reserved for the ascended masters that have conquered the cycles of time.

AND THOTH SAID
List ye, O man, drink of my wisdom.
Learn ye the secret that is Master of Time.
Learn ye how those ye call Masters are
able to remember the lives of the past.

Great is the secret yet easy to master,
giving to thee the mastery of time.
When upon thee death fast approaches,
fear not but know ye are master of Death.

Relax thy body, resist not with tension.
Place in thy heart the flame of thy Soul.

Swiftly then sweep it to the seat of the triangle.

Hold for a moment, then move to the goal.
This, thy goal, is the place between thine eyebrows,
the place where the memory of life must hold sway.
Hold thou thy flame here in thy brain-seat
until the fingers of Death grasp thy Soul.
Then as thou pass through the state of transition,
surely the memories of life shall pass, too.

Then shalt the past be as one with the present.
Then shall the memory of all be retained.
Free shalt thou be from all retrogression.
The things of the past shall live in today.

Thoth as revealed the method used to consciously incarnate. The pineal gland is the spiritual antenna that is the link between the transition from life to life. There is a famous verse in the Bible that references this: Genesis 32:30 "So Jacob called the place Peniel, saying, 'It is because I saw God face to face, and yet my life was spared.'" This is a profound statement. The only way out is "IN." We must take a journey to inner space. Only there will we find salvation.

ATLANTIS

Supplemental Tablet Fourteen

~ THE PLEIADIANS ~
"AS YOU COME INTO THE AGE OF LIGHT,
WORLDS WILL OPEN THAT YOU NEVER KNEW EXISTED."

AND THOTH SAID
List ye, O Man, to the deep hidden wisdom,
lost to the world since the time of the Dwellers,
lost and forgotten by men of this age.
Know ye this Earth is but a portal,
guarded by powers unknown to man.
Yet, the Dark Lords hide the entrance
that leads to the Heaven-born land.
Know ye, the way to the sphere of Arulu
is guarded by barriers opened only to Light-born man.

Upon Earth, I am the holder of the keys
to the gates of the Sacred Land.
Command I, by the powers beyond me,
to leave the keys to the world of man.
Before I depart, I give ye the Secrets of how
ye may rise from the bondage of darkness,
cast off the fetters of flesh that have bound ye,
rise from the darkness into the Light.

Know ye, the soul must be cleansed of its darkness,
ere ye may enter the portals of Light.
Thus, I established among ye the Mysteries
so that the Secrets may always be found.
Aye, though man may fall into darkness,
always the Light will shine as a guide.
Hidden in darkness, veiled in symbols,
always the way to the portal will be found.

Man in the future will deny the mysteries
but always the way the seeker will find.
Now I command ye to maintain my secrets,
giving only to those ye have tested,
so that the pure may not be corrupted,
so that the power of Truth may prevail.

List ye now to the unveiling of Mystery.
List to the symbols of Mystery I give.
Make of it a religion for only thus will its essence remain.
Regions there are two between
this life and the Great One,
traveled by the Souls
who depart from this Earth;

Duat, the home of the powers of illusion;
Sekhet Hetspet, the House of the Gods.

Osiris, the symbol of the guard of the portal,
who turns back the souls of unworthy men.
Beyond lies the sphere of the heaven-born powers,
Arulu, the land where the Great Ones have passed.

There, when my work among men has been finished,
will I join the Great Ones of my Ancient home.
Seven are the mansions of the house of the Mighty;
Three guards the portal of each house from the darkness;
Fifteen the ways that lead to Duat.
Twelve are the houses of the Lords of Illusion,
facing four ways, each of them different.
Forty and Two are the great powers,
judging the Dead who seek for the portal.
Four are the Sons of Horus,
Two are the Guards of East and West of Isis,
the mother who pleads for her children, Queen of the Moon,
reflecting the Sun.

Ba is the Essence, living forever.
Ka is the Shadow that man knows as life.
Ba cometh not until Ka is incarnate.
These are mysteries to preserve through the ages.
Keys are they of life and of Death.
Hear ye now the mystery of mysteries:
learn of the circle beginningless and endless,
the form of He who is One and in all.

Listen and hear it, go forth and apply it,
thus will ye travel the way that I go.
Mystery in Mystery,
yet clear to the Light-born,
the Secret of all I now will reveal.

I will declare a secret to the initiated,
but let the door be wholly shut against the profane.

Three is the mystery, come from the great one.
Hear, and Light on thee will dawn.
In the primeval, dwell three unities.
Other than these, none can exist.
These are the equilibrium, source of creation:
one God, one Truth, one point of freedom.
Three come forth from the three of the balance:
all life, all good, all power.

Three are the qualities of God in his Light-home:
Infinite power, Infinite Wisdom, Infinite Love.
Three are the powers given to the Masters:
To transmute evil, assist good, use discrimination.
Three are the things inevitable for God to perform:
Manifest power, wisdom and love.

Three are the powers creating all things:
Divine Love possessed of perfect knowledge,
Divine Wisdom knowing all possible means,
Divine Power possessed by the joint will of
Divine Love and Wisdom.
Three are the circles (states) of existence:
The circle of Light where dwells nothing but God,
and only God can traverse it;
the circle of Chaos where all things
by nature arise from death;
the Circle of awareness where
all things spring from life.

All things animate are of three states of existence:
chaos or death, liberty in humanity and felicity of Heaven.
Three necessities control all things:
beginning in the Great Deep,
the circle of chaos, plenitude in Heaven.
Three are the paths of the Soul:
Man, Liberty, Light.

Three are the hindrances:
lack of endeavor to obtain knowledge;
non-attachment to god; attachment to evil.

In man, the three are manifest.
Three are the Kings of power within.
Three are the chambers of the mysteries,
found yet not found in the body of man.
Hear ye now of he who is liberated,
freed from the bondage of life into Light.
Knowing the source of all worlds shall be open.
Aye, even the Gates of Arulu shall not be barred.
Yet heed, O man, who would'st enter heaven.
If ye be not worthy,
better it be to fall into the fire.

Know ye the celestials pass through the pure flame.
At every revolution of the heavens,
they bathe in the fountains of Light.

List ye, O man, to this mystery:
Long in the past before ye were man-born,
I dwelled in Ancient Atlantis.
There in the Temple,
I drank of the Wisdom,
poured as a fountain of Light
from the Dweller.

Give the key to ascend to the
Presence of Light in the Great world.
Stood I before the Holy One
enthroned in the Flower of Fire.
Veiled was he by the lightnings of darkness,
else my Soul by the Glory have been shattered.

Forth from the feet of his Throne like the diamond,

rolled forth four rivers of flame from his footstool,
rolled through the channels of clouds to the Man-world.
Filled was the hall with Spirits of Heaven.

Wonder of wonders was the Starry palace.
Above the sky, like a rainbow of Fire and Sunlight,
were Formed the Spirits.
Sang they the glories of the Holy One.
Then from the midst of the Fire came a voice:
Behold the Glory of the first Cause.

I beheld that Light, high above all darkness,
reflected in my own being.
I attained, as it were, to the God of all Gods,
the Spirit-Sun, the Sovereign of the Sun spheres.

There is One, Even the First,
who hath no beginning,
who hath no end;
who hath made all things,
who govern all,
who is good,
who is just,
who illumines,
who sustains.

Then from the throne, there poured a great radiance,
surrounding and lifting my soul by its power.
Swiftly I moved through the spaces of Heaven,
shown was I the mystery of mysteries,
shown the Secret heart of the cosmos.
Carried was I to the land of Arulu,
stood before the Lords in their Houses.

Opened they the Doorway so I might
glimpse the primeval chaos.

Shuddered my soul to the vision of horror,
shrank back my soul from the ocean of darkness.
Then saw I the need for the barriers,
saw the need for the Lords of Arulu..

Only they with their Infinite balance could
stand in the way of the inpouring chaos.
Only they could guard God's creation.
Then did I pass around the circle of eight.
Saw all the souls who had conquered the darkness.
Saw the splendor of Light where they dwelled.
Longed I to take my place in their circle,
but longed I also for the way I had chosen,
when I stood in the Halls of Amenti
and made my choice to the work I would do.

Passed I from the Halls of Arulu
down to the earth space where my body lay.
Arose I from the earth where I rested.

Stood I before the Dweller.
Gave my pledge to renounce my Great
right until my work on Earth was completed,
until the Age of darkness be past.

List ye, O man, to the words I shall give ye.
In them shall ye find the Essence of Life.
Before I return to the Halls of Amenti,
taught shall ye be the Secrets of Secrets,
how ye, too, may arise to the Light.

Preserve them and guard them,
hide them in symbols so the profane will laugh and renounce.
In every land, form ye the mysteries.
Make the way hard for the seeker to tread.
Thus will the weak and the wavering be rejected.

Thus will the secrets be hidden and guarded,
held till the time when the wheel shall be turned.

Through the dark ages, waiting and watching,
my Spirit shall remain in the deep hidden land.
When one has passed all the trials of the outer,
summon ye me by the Key that ye hold

Then will I, the Initiator, answer,
come from the Halls of the Gods in Amenti.
Then will I receive the initiate, give him the words of power.
Hark ye, remember, these words of warning:
bring not to me one lacking in wisdom,
impure in heart or weak in his purpose.
Else I will withdraw from ye your power
to summon me from the place of my sleeping.

Now go ye forth and summon thy brothers
so that I may impart the wisdom to light thy
path when my presence is gone.
Come to the chamber beneath my temple.
Eat not food until three days are past...

There will I give thee the essence of wisdom
so that with power ye may shine amongst men.
There will I give unto thee the secrets so that
ye, too, may rise to the
Heavens, God-men in Truth
as in essence ye be.
Depart now and leave me while I summon
those ye know of but as yet know not.

The "wheel will be turned..." "...the Key that you hold..." "...give unto thee the secrets so that ye too, may rise to the Heavens." Thoth has made extraordinary claims in this tablet regarding possible space travel. Extraordinary claims require extraordinary evidence. I decided to take a look into how we could open a stargate portal and if the ancients left any evidence behind, proving it might be possible. The evidence is both scientific and spiritual. When you combine the two you have unified physics.

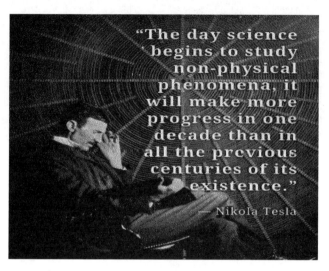

Tesla

Symbols, Pyramids, Quartz and other energies

"The Stargate portal is a device which opens a doorway in space and time and enables travelers to connect two distant realms or higher dimensions. NASA has discovered the portals exist naturally around the earth, accessing them with a device may, therefore. be much easier than first thought. Known as x-points, portals are born from the mingling of Earth's magnetic field with incoming solar winds. It is where the Sun and earth become connected by an uninterrupted path. These portals open and close a dozen times each day, magnetic reconnection via magnetic lines are forced from the Sun and Earth, crisscrossed and joined to create the opening. X-points are where the crisscross takes place, in essence, these are wormholes in space." Reference for this information: https://www.nasa.gov/mission_pages/sunearth/news/mag-portals.html and https://science.nasa.gov/science-news/science-at-nasa/2012/29jun_hiddenportals

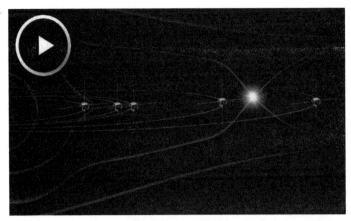

Image Credit – Public Record, Science At NASA – X-Points VIDEO: https://
science.nasa.gov/science-news/science-at-nasa/2012/29jun_hiddenportals

Image Credit – Sociedelic – Bosnian Pyramid Of The Sun

Pyramids have long been associated with being used as stargates for pharaohs after death. The word 'pyramid' comes from the prefix 'pyra-,' meaning fire and the suffix '-mid,' meaning middle. When combined, they form the concept of 'fire in the middle.' Author Patrick Flanagan's book, *Pyramid Power: The Millennium Science*, illustrates the five angles that the pyramid projects as a beam of radiation toward the center into what he refers to as bio cosmic energy. Mathematically, it is the geometric center of the pyramid. Dan Davidson spent thirty-five years of research into finding how shapes and different materials convert into other forces and energies. In his book, *Shape Power*, a pyramid shape acts like a lens focusing the Earth's magnetism. The reason the pyramid shape is the best of focusing energy in this way is because on the atomic level, the abundant element carbon, which is the basis of all known life in the universe. Also read: https://www.ancient-code.com/secret-power-pyramidal-shape/

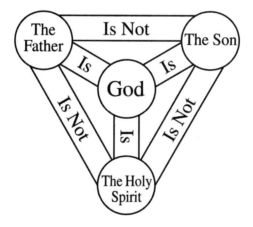

According to Joe Parr's research, (http://www.gizapyramid.com/parr/Index.html), "during the 12th century the shield of the Trinity diagram orientated the triangle upside down while a related Tetragrammaton put the face of God in the center, as churches all over Europe used this symbol. In the fifth Chapel of the Palace of Versailles France a Tetragrammaton has a triangle with the four-letter name of God written in Hebrew in the center and enclosed by a circle, while the circle represents unbroken perfect symmetry. The energy bubble the pyramid creates when it is energized is defined by Marco Roden as a torus, as seen in the below illustration.

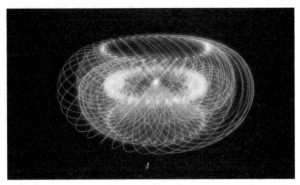

A Torus Construction

"In either case, it represents the physical manifestation of energy in three spatial dimensions, one of the more profound representations of the fire in the middle concept is derived from the detractors of this ten-point pyramid. The ten-point pyramid is arranged in four rows and believed by Pythagoreans to be at the root of all nature. The capstone or top point was considered to be divine as it alone touches the heavens. Each row of numbers represents a different spatial dimension from one of the four elements while pairs of rows could be radius musical ratios. The Tetractys embraces within itself in seed like form the principles of the natural world, the harmony of the cosmos, the assent to the divine, and the mysteries of the divine realm." Also Read: J. Wilkinson's *Tetragrammaton: Western Christians and the Hebrew Name of God: From the Beginnings to the Seventeenth Century* (2015).

Fifth Chapel of the Palace of Versailles.Credit image: P. Vasiliadis

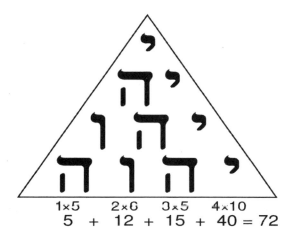

1×5   2×6   3×5   4×10
5   +   12   +   15   +   40 = 72

Image Credit - Wikipedia - Tetragrammaton Tetractys

"The Kabbalah uses a tetragrammaton tetractys to manifest the 72 emanations of God. According to the Kabbalah, mankind must climb the tetragrammaton through spiritual healing in order to reunite with the Creator. Both the seed of life and Marko Rodin's fingerprint of God can be combined with Pythagoras' ten-point tetractys. This perfect fit between mathematics, music, and geometry and has already been extended into the discipline of physics." https://capstone.pw/how-to-open-a-stargate-portal380773.htm.

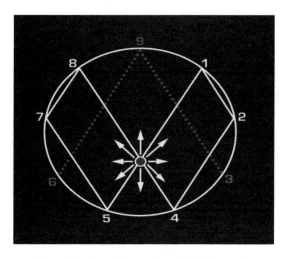

Marko Rodin's Vortex Based Mathematics

"The Higgs Boson, which gives mass to the 16 elementary particles, is inscribed as a circle, while the photon is inscribed as a hexagon. Six quarks in a standard hexagon model are an indication of the higher dimensions of space. Coincidentally, a Stargate requires six points to define an address or location in three-dimensional space. Time is also considered as an extra dimension." The link for learning more about this subject is: https://www.scientificamerican.com/article/what-exactly-is-the-higgs/

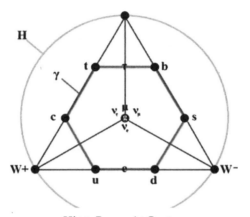

Higgs Boson At Center

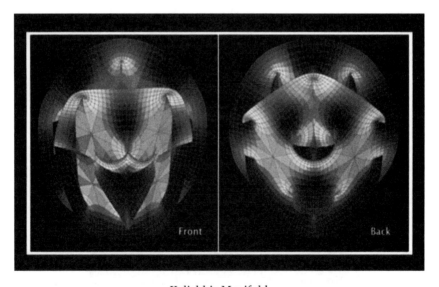

Kaliabhia Manifold

"What is more amazing is how the Kaliabhia Manifold resembles the two-headed God; a God of duality like harmony and chaos or possibly the outer and inner world which are separated from being united together. In quantum physics, there is wave particle duality. If this six-dimensional manifold of duality is put into the tetractys in place of the six points that make up a hexagon, a familiar image emerges, a sphinx sitting in front of a pyramid.

"The tetractys with Kaliabhia manifold overlay represents mankind's desire to join with God by overcoming the duality created by the lower human self which feels separated from the higher spiritual self. The seed of life is formed from seven circles being placed with six-fold symmetry, forming a pattern of circles and lenses. To a religious person, it depicts the six days of creation. To a physicist, it represents lines of interference of the triple envelope from a sympathetic resonance. To a mathematician, three points of propagation form a vertex for a triangle, where the circular waves are weaved becomes its geometric center. To a Thermite, all six points of propagation form a unicursal hexagon with a five petaled flower in the center symbolizing a pentacle. To a practitioner of magic, it represents a planetary hexagram with the Sun representing true will in the center. To an enlightened person, all six points of propagation form a Merkabah or vehicle of Ascension. The fire in the middle of the Merkabah is the navel chakra or sacral plexus near the navel area. It is associated with the womb or center of creation."
http://www.ascensionnow.co.uk/star-tetrahedron-merkaba.html

Tetractys with Kaliabhia manifold overlay

As you study this information, you will notice an interesting fact in your research of the Kabbalah, the pyramid, and others concerning secret symbols. The following online URL is listed as a PDF document with the title: **[PDF]**Secret Teachings of All Ages Index - CIA. (Yes, referring to the infamous CIA). If you click on that designation, the search will bring up the words: COULDN'T OPEN PDF. Return to the original page and copy/paste the secondary URL, which is https://www.cia.gov/.../ E4AAFF6DAF6863F459A8B4E52DFB9FF4_Manly.P.Hall_/   Upon searching there you will find the words: The page you requested does not exist on CIA.gov. However, it is common knowledge that the CIA has released millions of declassified documents over the last twenty years. For decades, this vital information was kept hidden from the general population. Now the information has been literally dumped in such voluminous disorganization that, finding the documents released can be an overwhelming tasks.

Finding serious documentation about our subjects continues to require those interested to volunteer their time to pour over the mountain of data available. I challenge all who are interested to devote time and energy to locating and making available anything that pertains to our studies that had been previously catalogued by the CIA. The CIA does sponsor a reading room, however, it is highly selected documents, many of which have been 'sanitized.' They do have a few interesting documents released concerning UFO's and from this website you can navigate to other unsanitized and sanitized documents. Ostensibly missing, however, are documents referring to symbols of ancient mysteries. https://www.cia.gov/news-information/blog/2016/take-a-peek-into-our-x-files.html

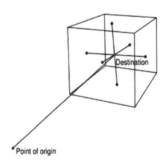

Image Credit 4biddenknowledge The Holy Grail: Divine Coordinates

Stone circles also have the power to concentrate vibrational energy into the middle or center. The most well-known stone circle is Stonehenge near Amesbury. The outer ring of sarsen stones are made up of high silica sandstone, which is composed of quartz. Quartz crystals have a piezoelectric quality. The asymmetry of its atomic groups make silica an effective transducer for converting mechanical energy into electrical energy. Sound waves are mechanical energy. The sarsens trilithons behave as tuning forks. In fact, the trilithons could be thought of as tuning fork crystals. A tuning fork oscillator will resonate close to its target frequency according to how it was cut. They therefore could keep an ultrasonic beam steady for communication. If a spherical stone was placed in the center of Stonehenge, it could act as an optical lens or radio receiver for the sympathetic resonances created between the trilithons.

Image Credit 4biddenknowledge – Merkaba – Sacral Chakra – Naval Plexus

"In 2012, several blue stones tested at the site of the Bosnian Pyramid sounded like metallic bells drums, and gongs. A sacred chant of specific tones causes all the surrounding stones to resonate. Constructive and destructive interference patterns form around the stones. Somatic experiments held in the King's Chamber of the Pyramid of Giza in 1997 by John Stuart Reid showed how the Eye of Horus symbol appeared as a vibrate channel turned within the sarcophagus. When struck, the sarcophagus sounds like a gong due to its two-to-one ratio.

"On the back of a Federal Reserve Note, the Eye of Providence or all-seeing eye is centered on the capstone of a 13-step pyramid. It is also centered on the black pyramid of Ecuador found in the 1980s. What is the significance of the eye being inserted into the capstone? The capstone is the most important piece of a pyramid. Made of the right granite or fine limestone and often covered in gold leaf, it focused the energy of the pyramid like a lens. When pyramids are built, they are completed up to the final capstone. The capstone, which is a single piece of stone, is then lowered into position. It is squared on the bottom in order to fit snugly into place. Once placed on top of a pyramid, it allowed an open connection into higher dimensions or spiritual realm.

"The Bosnian pyramid of the Sun is a fully operational Stargate, opening it will require great care. The capstone and quartz still need to be in place for the pyramid to focus its correct resonating frequency. The human body must also be put into proper vibration by way of meditation. Since pyramids are tuned to human frequencies, the human body must also be tuned to them in order to travel through the Stargate." https://capstone.pw/how-to-open-a-stargate-portal380773.html

K2 Megalith – Bosnian Pyramid

You will also want to read more about the amazing findings at the Pyramid of the Sun and Moon in Bosnia: https://etheric.com/bosnian-pyramid-complex-signs-technically-advanced-ice-age-civilization/

Image Credit Bosnianpyramid.com

CHAPTER SEVENTEEN

SECRETS OF SECRETS

Supplemental Tablet Fifteen

Tablet 15 is a supplemental tablet. This tablet teaches the ascension to the God-Man by receiving the "Ba," as well as the Yin and Yang nature of the Universe and how it relates to entropy and order forms chaos.

AND THOTH SAID
Now ye assemble, my children,
waiting to hear the Secret of Secrets
which shall give ye power to unfold the God-man,
give ye the way to Eternal life.

Plainly shall I speak of the Unveiled Mysteries.
No dark sayings shall I give unto thee.
Open thine ears now, my children.
Hear and obey the words that I give.

First I shall speak of the fetters of darkness
which bind ye in chains to the sphere of the Earth.

Darkness and light are both of one nature,
different only in seeming,
for each arose from the source of all.
Darkness is disorder.
Light is Order.
Darkness transmuted is light of the Light.
This, my children, your purpose in being;
transmutation of darkness to light.

Hear ye now of the mystery of nature,

the relations of life to the Earth where it dwells.
Know ye, ye are threefold in nature,
physical, astral and mental in one.

Three are the qualities of each of the natures;
nine in all, as above, so below.

In the physical are these channels,
the blood which moves in vortical motion,
reacting on the heart to continue its beating.
Magnetism which moves through the nerve paths,
carrier of energies to all cells and tissues.
Akasa which flows through channels,
subtle yet physical, completing the channels.

Each of the three attuned with each other,
each affecting the life of the body.
Form they the skeletal framework through
which the subtle ether flows.
In their mastery lies the Secret of Life in the body.
Relinquished only by will of the adept,
when his purpose in living is done.

Three are the natures of the Astral,
mediator is between above and below;
not of the physical, not of the Spiritual,
but able to move above and below.

Three are the natures of Mind,
carrier it of the Will of the Great One.
Arbitrator of Cause and Effect in thy life.
Thus is formed the threefold being,
directed from above by the power of four.

Above and beyond man's threefold nature
lies the realm of the Spiritual Self. Four is it in qualities,

shining in each of the planes of existence,
but thirteen in one,
the mystical number.

Based on the qualities of man are the Brothers:
each shall direct the unfoldment of being,
each shall channels be of the Great One.

On Earth, man is in bondage,
bound by space and time to the earth plane.
Encircling each planet, a wave of vibration,
binds him to his plane of unfoldment.
Yet within man is the Key to releasement,
within man may freedom be found.

Image Courtesy of – 4biddenknowledge – Billy Carson

Thoth clearly references Earth and all other planets where men reside
as prison planets. Energetically, the spirit of all men are bound to his/
her planet in a temporal prison (avatar body). Only the adept can break
the cycle of reincarnation back in the same energetic field.

AND THOTH SAID

When ye have released the self from the body,
rise to the outermost bounds of your earth-plane.
Speak ye the word Dor-E-Lil-La.

Then for a time your Light will be lifted,
free may ye pass the barriers of space.
For a time of half of the sun (six hours),
free may ye pass the barriers of earth-plane,
see and know those who are beyond thee.

Thoth is setting the pace of Astral Exploration for the reader. By saying the words, "Dor-E-Lil-La," astral projection can be achieved.

AND THOTH SAID

Yea, to the highest worlds may ye pass.
See your own possible heights of unfoldment,
know all earthly futures of Soul.

Bound are ye in your body,
but by the power ye may be free.
This is the Secret whereby bondage
shall be replaced by freedom for thee.

Calm let thy mind be.
At rest be thy body:
Conscious only of freedom from flesh.
Center thy being on the goal of thy longing.
Think over and over that thou wouldst be free.
Think of this word La-Um-I-L-Ganoover
and over in thy mind let it sound.
Drift with the sound to the place of thy longing.
Free from the bondage of flesh by thy will.

The last stanza provides the protocol for obtaining a successful Astral Projection.

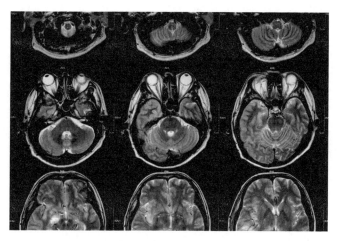

Image Courtesy of – 4biddenknowledge – Billy Carson

Many of you have heard of those who claim they have had out-of-body experiences (a.k.a. astral travel), where they float outside of their bodies and see themselves from the outside. Perhaps you've experienced this phenomenon for yourself. Did you know there are those who can astral travel at will? A team of scientists scanned the brain of a woman who could do just that. What they found was remarkable.

The scientists names are Andra M. Smith and Claude Messier from the University of Ottawa. In their paper published in "Frontiers of Human Neuroscience," they describe the subject's ability and how her brain reacted during her astral trip.

What they found was that her visual cortex deactivated, while the left side of several areas associated with kinesthetic imagery activated, which is the part of the brain that allows people to interact with the world.

To read about the finer details of their work, follow the link below:
https://sploid.gizmodo.com/scientists-unlock-mystery-of-woman-who-sees-herself-out-1538196076

AND THOTH SAID

Hear ye while I give the greatest of secrets:
how ye may enter the Halls of Amenti,
enter the place of the immortals as I did,
stand before the Lords in their places.

Lie ye down in rest of thy body.
Calm thy mind so no thought disturbs thee.
Pure must ye be in mind and in purpose,
else only failure will come unto thee.

Vision Amenti as I have told in my Tablets.
Long with fullness of heart to be there.
Stand before the Lords in thy mind's eye.

Pronounce the words of power I give;
Mekut-El-Shab-El Hale-Sur-Ben-El-Zabrut Zin-Efrim-Quar-El.

Relax thy mind and thy body.
Then be sure your soul will be called.

Now give I the Key to Shambhala,
the place where my Brothers live in the darkness:
Darkness but filled with Light of the Sun
Darkness of Earth, but Light of the Spirit,
guides for ye when my day is done.

Image Courtesy of– 4biddenknowledge – Billy Carson

Shambhala

Several ancint texts from various traditions mention beings from
'another world' that exist within our own. One such world, referenced in
Tibetan Buddhist and Hindu traditions, is Shambhala, which is a hidden

kingdom within our own planet, a place which we do not understand and is difficult to find.

Shambhala is circular, yet is depicted as an eight-petalled lotus blossom—a symbol of the heart Chakra. Although this may be seen as a magical, mythical, and unique place, it is not alone. Many ancient cultures and texts have accepted the existence of such mysterious lands. It's especially fascinating to see how much of the ancient writings of Buddhism, Vedic philosophy, and Eastern traditions are now being confirmed by modern science. For example: the conundrum of consciousness directly correlates with quantum physics and goes hand in hand with the existence of other realms. Perhaps researching ancient Eastern philosophies is where some of Nikola Tesla's ideas came from. On a similar note, did you know that most of our pioneering scientists were mystics?

Read more here: http://www.theeventchronicle.com/metaphysics/spiritual/legend-shambhala-hidden-land-exists-within

AND THOTH SAID

Leave thou thy body as I have taught thee.
Pass to the barriers of the deep, hidden place.
Stand before the gates and their guardians.
Command thy entrance by these words:

I am the Light. In me is no darkness.
Free am I of the bondage of night.
Open thou the way of the Twelve and the One,
so I may pass to the realm of wisdom.

When they refuse thee, as surely they will,
command them to open by these words of power:
I am the Light. For me are no barriers.
Open, I command, by the Secret of Secrets
Edom-El-Ahim-Sabbert-Zur Adom.

Then if thy words have been Truth of the highest,
open for thee the barriers will fall.

Now, I leave thee, my children.
Down, yet up, to the Halls shall I go.
Win ye the way to me, my children.
Truly my brothers shall ye become.

Thus finish I my writings.
Keys let them be to those who come after.
But only to those who seek my wisdom,

for only for these am I the Key and the Way.

Jesus answered, "I am the way and the truth and the life. No one comes to the Father except through me." John 14:6

There are so many similarities between what Thoth wrote and what claimed to be said by Yeshua also known as Jesus. The Biblical text was written between 100 AD to 900 AD. The Emerald Tablets were written over 36,000 years ago. Yet, so much of the content is virtually the same. The writers of the Bible were huge followers of Hermes also known as Thoth. I hypothesize that this is why there are so many similarities. They literally copied most of the biblical content from the Emerald Tablets.

Message from the author: Thank you for reading my book. I look forward to seeing you in the astral plane.

Image credit Pantheon Elite Records - Emerald Tablets by Donny Arcade ft
4biddenknowledge – Anjolique and Layzie Bone

Acknowledgements

Writing this book was a dream manifested into reality. From the moment I learned of Thoth, I felt and instant connection. The more I studied his work the more I began to take on fractals of his consciousness. This is one of the biggest secrets of the mystery schools. We can all live through others by transferring our knowledge into new minds. By this method we use the fractal network to propagate information, knowledge and ideas.

I would like to thank Thoth. Master of all arts and sciences, perfect in all crafts, Ruler of the Three Worlds, Scribe of the Gods, and Keeper of the Books of Life,

Thoth Hermes Trismegistus—the Three Times Greatest, the "First Intelligencer."

I would like to thank myself for putting in 45 years of hard work and dedication backed by real research and investigation into ancient history, metaphysics, quantum physics, astronomy, anthropology, biology, and aerospace.

I would like to thank Jimmy Church and his beautiful wife, Rita. From day number one, Jimmy Church Radio and Coast To Coast AM have supported my work and believed in me. Jimmy, I can't thank you and the Fadernaughts enough! Thank you for writing the Forward for this book and thank you for being a part of my journey. Love you brother!

Special thanks to George Noory for his unwavering support. I appreciate the interviews on Beyond Belief and Coast To Coast AM.

I would like to thank Gaia.com for supporting my work and giving me the opportunity to showcase my knowledge on their conscious streaming network. Special thanks to Deb Moore, Jirka Rysavy, Sid Goldberg, Jay Weidner, Melissa Tittl, Tucker Collins and everyone at Gaia that believed in my abilities.

I would like to thank Laura Cantu of Winterwolf Press. Laura you believed in my mission and helped to lead me in the right direction. I appreciate you and your team so much!!!

I would like to thank my children Jordan, April, Bobbi, Giovanni, and Justin for letting me be me. They have also been both my students and my teachers. Special thanks to my grandchildren Skylar and Johnathan.

I would like to thank the Anunnaki History team: Bianca Leonhard, Thomas Mickey Jensen, Dollie Leanne-Dawn Jensen, Tina Salt, Jj Ainsworth, Cornelius Lester Tony Lytollis, Dominic Joyce, Ed Parker, Nikki Reyna, James Tracy, Alex Teplish, Renee Molinary, Rana Nefatari Wieland, and Maria Conceiçao Prazeres Coelho.

I would like to thank the United Family Of Anomaly Hunters team: Thomas Mikey Jensen, Martine Grainey, Chris Moroney, Neville Thompson, Dollie Leanne Deeming Jensen, Bianca Leonhard, Dominic Joyce, Gerald Turner, Joe White, James Tracy, Miša Drezgie, Brian Hopjins, Will Farrar, and Rami Bar Illan.

Special thanks to...

- Dr. Tara Swart; M.I.T. Professor and author of The Source (Change Your Life).

- Jaden Smith; Accomplished actor, rapper and son of Will Smith. Chris Brown; Multi platinum artist and actor.

- Jimmy Church; of JimmyChurchRadio.com, iHeart Radio and Coast To Coast AM.

- George Noory; Of Coast To Coast AM and iHeart Radio. Erich Von Daniken; Best Selling Author of Chariots Of The Gods and TV Host.

- Donny Arcade; Billboard artist and actor.

- Victor Rival; Life Coach and fitness trainer and dear friend.

- Bizzie Gold; It was both a pleasure and an honor to share knowledge and consciousness transformation techniques with Bizzie Gold

- CrewZ; Music artist and song writer

A special Thank You to everyone that has supported my work over the years.

THE LAST WORDS OF THRICE-GREAT HERMES

Wise words, although written by my decaying hand, remain imperishable through time; imbued with the medicine of immortality by the All-Master.
Be unseen and undiscovered by all those who will come and go, wandering the wastelands of life. Be hidden, until an older heaven births human beings who are worthy of your wisdom.'